College English for Art Majors

艺术类
大学英语 ①

教师用书

总主编　余渭深

主　编　朱万忠　韩　萍

副主编　杨晓斌　李文英

编　者　（按姓氏笔画排列）

王　艳　兰　橙　朱万忠　李文英　何　冰

杨晓斌　林海明　梅玉华　韩　萍

Teacher's Book

重庆大学出版社

内 容 提 要

《艺术类大学英语1教师用书》是《艺术类大学英语1》的配套教师参考用书。全书共8个单元,分别对应主教材8个主题单元。内容除了提供基本的练习答案和课文翻译以外,还包括主题课文相关背景知识的详细延伸介绍、课文长难句分析、重点词汇及语法讲解。该书内容详实,符合任课老师的课堂教学需要。为了适应当下的多媒体课堂教学的特点,本教师用书还配有课件光盘,方便任课教师备课和组织课堂活动。

图书在版编目(CIP)数据

艺术类大学英语(1)教师用书/朱万忠主编. —
重庆:重庆大学出版社,2011.7
艺术类大学英语系列教材
ISBN 978-7-5624-6210-1

Ⅰ.①艺… Ⅱ.①朱… Ⅲ.①艺术—英语—高等学校
—教学参考资料 Ⅳ.①H31

中国版本图书馆 CIP 数据核字(2011)第 110541 号

艺术类大学英语1 教师用书

主 编 朱万忠 韩 萍

责任编辑:牟 妮 版式设计:牟 妮
责任校对:谢 芳 责任印制:赵 晟

*

重庆大学出版社出版发行
出版人:邓晓益
社址:重庆市沙坪坝正街 174 号重庆大学(A 区)内
邮编:400030
电话:(023) 65102378 65105781
传真:(023) 65103686 65105565
网址:http://www.cqup.com.cn
邮箱:fxk@cqup.com.cn(营销中心)
全国新华书店经销
重庆升光电力印务有限公司印刷

*

开本:889×1194 1/16 印张:8 字数:248 千
2011 年 7 月第 1 版 2011 年 7 月第 1 次印刷
ISBN 978-7-5624-6210-1 定价:48.00 元(含 1 教学光盘)

目 录

Unit 1　Musicians ⋯⋯⋯⋯⋯⋯⋯⋯⋯⋯⋯⋯⋯⋯⋯⋯⋯⋯⋯⋯⋯⋯⋯ 1

　Ⅰ. Background Information ⋯⋯⋯⋯⋯⋯⋯⋯⋯⋯⋯⋯⋯⋯⋯⋯⋯ 1

　Ⅱ. Notes ⋯⋯⋯⋯⋯⋯⋯⋯⋯⋯⋯⋯⋯⋯⋯⋯⋯⋯⋯⋯⋯⋯⋯⋯⋯ 2

　Ⅲ. Language Points ⋯⋯⋯⋯⋯⋯⋯⋯⋯⋯⋯⋯⋯⋯⋯⋯⋯⋯⋯⋯ 5

　Ⅳ. Keys, Tapescripts and Text Translations ⋯⋯⋯⋯⋯⋯⋯⋯ 10

Unit 2　Painters ⋯⋯⋯⋯⋯⋯⋯⋯⋯⋯⋯⋯⋯⋯⋯⋯⋯⋯⋯⋯⋯⋯⋯⋯ 17

　Ⅰ. Background Information ⋯⋯⋯⋯⋯⋯⋯⋯⋯⋯⋯⋯⋯⋯⋯⋯⋯ 17

　Ⅱ. Notes ⋯⋯⋯⋯⋯⋯⋯⋯⋯⋯⋯⋯⋯⋯⋯⋯⋯⋯⋯⋯⋯⋯⋯⋯⋯ 17

　Ⅲ. Language Points ⋯⋯⋯⋯⋯⋯⋯⋯⋯⋯⋯⋯⋯⋯⋯⋯⋯⋯⋯⋯ 19

　Ⅳ. Keys, Tapescripts and Text Translations ⋯⋯⋯⋯⋯⋯⋯⋯ 24

Unit 3　Actors and Actresses ⋯⋯⋯⋯⋯⋯⋯⋯⋯⋯⋯⋯⋯⋯⋯⋯ 31

　Ⅰ. Background Information ⋯⋯⋯⋯⋯⋯⋯⋯⋯⋯⋯⋯⋯⋯⋯⋯⋯ 31

　Ⅱ. Notes ⋯⋯⋯⋯⋯⋯⋯⋯⋯⋯⋯⋯⋯⋯⋯⋯⋯⋯⋯⋯⋯⋯⋯⋯⋯ 32

　Ⅲ. Language Points ⋯⋯⋯⋯⋯⋯⋯⋯⋯⋯⋯⋯⋯⋯⋯⋯⋯⋯⋯⋯ 36

　Ⅳ. Keys, Tapescripts and Text Translations ⋯⋯⋯⋯⋯⋯⋯⋯ 40

Unit 4　Dancers ⋯⋯⋯⋯⋯⋯⋯⋯⋯⋯⋯⋯⋯⋯⋯⋯⋯⋯⋯⋯⋯⋯⋯⋯ 45

　Ⅰ. Background Information ⋯⋯⋯⋯⋯⋯⋯⋯⋯⋯⋯⋯⋯⋯⋯⋯⋯ 45

　Ⅱ. Notes ⋯⋯⋯⋯⋯⋯⋯⋯⋯⋯⋯⋯⋯⋯⋯⋯⋯⋯⋯⋯⋯⋯⋯⋯⋯ 46

　Ⅲ. Language Points ⋯⋯⋯⋯⋯⋯⋯⋯⋯⋯⋯⋯⋯⋯⋯⋯⋯⋯⋯⋯ 48

　Ⅳ. Keys, Tapescripts and Text Translations ⋯⋯⋯⋯⋯⋯⋯⋯ 52

Unit 5　Designers ⋯⋯⋯⋯⋯⋯⋯⋯⋯⋯⋯⋯⋯⋯⋯⋯⋯⋯⋯⋯⋯⋯⋯ 61

　Ⅰ. Background Information ⋯⋯⋯⋯⋯⋯⋯⋯⋯⋯⋯⋯⋯⋯⋯⋯⋯ 61

　Ⅱ. Notes ⋯⋯⋯⋯⋯⋯⋯⋯⋯⋯⋯⋯⋯⋯⋯⋯⋯⋯⋯⋯⋯⋯⋯⋯⋯ 62

　Ⅲ. Language Points ⋯⋯⋯⋯⋯⋯⋯⋯⋯⋯⋯⋯⋯⋯⋯⋯⋯⋯⋯⋯ 65

　Ⅳ. Keys, Tapescripts and Text Translations ⋯⋯⋯⋯⋯⋯⋯⋯ 69

Unit 6　Famous Singers ⋯⋯⋯⋯⋯⋯⋯⋯⋯⋯⋯⋯⋯⋯⋯⋯⋯⋯⋯ 75

　Ⅰ. Background Information ⋯⋯⋯⋯⋯⋯⋯⋯⋯⋯⋯⋯⋯⋯⋯⋯⋯ 75

　Ⅱ. Notes ⋯⋯⋯⋯⋯⋯⋯⋯⋯⋯⋯⋯⋯⋯⋯⋯⋯⋯⋯⋯⋯⋯⋯⋯⋯ 76

　Ⅲ. Language Points ⋯⋯⋯⋯⋯⋯⋯⋯⋯⋯⋯⋯⋯⋯⋯⋯⋯⋯⋯⋯ 81

　Ⅳ. Keys, Tapescripts and Text Translations ⋯⋯⋯⋯⋯⋯⋯⋯ 84

Unit 7　Photographers ⋯⋯⋯⋯⋯⋯⋯⋯⋯⋯⋯⋯⋯⋯⋯⋯⋯⋯⋯⋯ 92

　Ⅰ. Background Information ⋯⋯⋯⋯⋯⋯⋯⋯⋯⋯⋯⋯⋯⋯⋯⋯⋯ 92

　Ⅱ. Notes ⋯⋯⋯⋯⋯⋯⋯⋯⋯⋯⋯⋯⋯⋯⋯⋯⋯⋯⋯⋯⋯⋯⋯⋯⋯ 92

　Ⅲ. Language Points ⋯⋯⋯⋯⋯⋯⋯⋯⋯⋯⋯⋯⋯⋯⋯⋯⋯⋯⋯⋯ 96

　Ⅳ. Keys, Tapescripts and Text Translations ⋯⋯⋯⋯⋯⋯⋯ 102

Unit 8　Playwrights ⋯⋯⋯⋯⋯⋯⋯⋯⋯⋯⋯⋯⋯⋯⋯⋯⋯⋯⋯⋯ 108

　Ⅰ. Background Information ⋯⋯⋯⋯⋯⋯⋯⋯⋯⋯⋯⋯⋯⋯⋯⋯ 108

　Ⅱ. Notes ⋯⋯⋯⋯⋯⋯⋯⋯⋯⋯⋯⋯⋯⋯⋯⋯⋯⋯⋯⋯⋯⋯⋯⋯ 108

　Ⅲ. Language Points ⋯⋯⋯⋯⋯⋯⋯⋯⋯⋯⋯⋯⋯⋯⋯⋯⋯⋯⋯ 112

　Ⅳ. Keys, Tapescripts and Text Translations ⋯⋯⋯⋯⋯⋯⋯ 116

Unit 1　Musicians

I. Background Information

Music is an expression of emotion. A musician is a person who writes, performs, or makes music. Musicians can be classified by their roles in creating or performing music.

◆ An instrumentalist plays a musical instrument.

◆ A multi-instrumentalist plays a diverse range of instruments such as different forms of percussion, plucked strings, vocals etc.

◆ A singer is a vocalist.

◆ Composers, songwriters and arrangers create musical compositions, songs and arrangements. These may be transcribed in music notation, performed or recorded.

◆ A conductor leads a musical ensemble. A conductor can simultaneously act as an instrumentalist in the ensemble.

◆ A recording artist creates recorded music, such as CDs and MP3 files.

Many people have dreamed of becoming musicians. Some have natural talent while others have to work harder to master some techniques. Being a musician isn't that challenging, although it's not easy either. It requires commitment, practice, and inspiration. If you follow the steps below, you too have a chance of becoming a great musician!

◆ Buy an instrument, but pick something you fancy. Perhaps you dream of rocking out on a guitar; perhaps you dream of banging on the drums; or maybe you want to try the tuba. Your first instrument is an extension of yourself, so choose carefully.

◆ Learn music theory. To some people, music theory seems like a waste of time. However, music theory is one of the most important parts of playing as well as composing music. Music theory can be learned through books and internet, although you may have more success with a tutor or by attending a musical school. Most musical schools do not require you to go there every day, and they do not interfere with your regular life. Also, learn musical history. Learn about different instruments and pieces from different composers. Be sure to listen to a lot of music and pay attention to specific techniques and ways to play an instrument.

◆ You'll improve quickly and have fun fairly soon, then you'll realize the need to play with other people, to learn musical theory, and, trust me, you'll feel far less bored learning scales and chords.

◆ Just enjoy!

◆ Learn to read music. While you can play by ear, it can be good if you can learn how to read sheet music. Learn all of the notes and practice a lot on the piano; then, learn how to sight read. Sight reading is also a very valuable skill. Many beginners as well as intermediates have trouble reading music, so be sure to practice a lot!

II. Notes

1. Notes to Lead-in

乐曲简介:《土耳其进行曲》全称为《"土耳其进行曲"主题变奏曲》,这是一首以"土耳其进行曲"为主题而驰名世界的变奏曲。实际上,本曲的主题本身并非具有纯正的土耳其风格,只是反映了当时流行的一种"东方风格",而在现代人看来,本曲几乎没有什么东方味道。但是由于它具有十分通俗而流畅的旋律,故成为不朽的古典小品。乐曲的主题简洁而极其节奏化,八分音符均为一贯的节奏,加上十六分音符来提高活泼感,全曲表现出一种带有童贞般的单纯(片段1)。像这种快活的节奏,在莫扎特的作品中屡见不鲜。各个变奏并不着力渲染技巧,但朴实有力,而又不陷于单调,是一种巧妙的关联。

2. Notes to Module 1

(1) Meishi Film Academy

美视电影学院。美视电影学院是重庆大学直属的27个学院之一,于2000年经教育部批准、由重庆大学与香港美视电力集团合作创立。学院现设有表演、播音与主持艺术、导演、戏剧影视文学、广播电视编导、摄影、戏剧影视美术设计及服装和化妆设计等8个本科专业(方向),学院拥有电影学硕士学位授权点,全院现有在校本科生近1 000名;硕士研究生60余名;重庆大学特聘著名演员、导演、制片人张国立为学院院长。

(2) Johann Sebastian Bach

约翰·塞巴斯蒂安·巴赫(1685年3月21日—1750年7月28日)巴洛克时期的德国作曲家,杰出的管风琴、小提琴、大键琴演奏家。巴赫被普遍认为是音乐史上最重要的作曲家之一,他的创作使用了德国丰富的音乐风格和娴熟的复调技巧;他的音乐集成了巴洛克音乐风格的精华,并被尊称为西方"现代音乐"之父,也是西方文化史上最重要的人物之一。

(3) Jakob Ludwig Felix Mendelssohn Bartholdy

雅科布·路德维希·费利克斯·门德尔松·巴托尔迪(1809年2月3日—1847年11月4日),德国犹太裔作曲家,为德国浪漫乐派最具代表性的人物之一,被誉为浪漫主义杰出的"抒情风景画大师",作品以精美、优雅、华丽著称。

(4) Frédéric Francois Chopin

弗雷德里克·弗朗西斯克·肖邦(1810年3月1日—1849年10月17日),伟大的波兰音乐家,欧洲19世纪浪漫主义音乐的代表人物。年少成名,后半生正值波兰亡国,在国外渡过,创作了很多具有爱国主义思想的钢琴作品,以此抒发自己的思乡情、亡国恨。其一生不离钢琴,被称为"钢琴诗人"。1837年严辞拒绝沙俄授予他的"俄国皇帝陛下首席钢琴家"的职位。舒曼称他的音乐像"藏在花丛中的一尊大炮",向全世界宣告"波兰不会亡"。肖邦晚年生活非常孤寂,痛苦地自称是"远离母亲的波兰孤儿"。他临终嘱咐亲人把自己的心脏运回祖国。

（5）The Church of the Holy Cross

波兰圣十字大教堂位于波兰首都华沙市中心，它的命运与这座城市乃至整个波兰民族的命运紧密相连。现在的圣十字大教堂是战争硝烟散去后 1946 年重建的巴罗克式建筑。在这座圣堂里，肖邦曾不止一次地做过祈祷。肖邦临终时将不能身返祖国视为终生憾事，嘱咐亲人将他的心脏一定要运回祖国。遵照他的遗嘱，人们将他的心脏运到了波兰华沙，安放在圣十字大教堂。

3. Notes to Module 2

（1）Bonn

波恩。德国历史古城波恩，位于莱茵河中游两岸，北距科隆市 21 公里，扼莱茵河上游山地和下游平原的咽喉，地理位置重要，历史上为战略要地。

（2）Vienna

维也纳。奥地利首都，同时也是奥地利的九个联邦州之一，是奥地利最大的城市和政治中心，位于多瑙河畔。维也纳约有 165 万人口，在欧盟城市中居第 10 位。维也纳是联合国的四个官方驻地之一，除此之外维也纳也是石油输出国组织、欧洲安全与合作组织和国际原子能机构的总部以及其他国际机构的所在地。

（3）Salzburg

萨尔斯堡（奥地利城市）。是奥地利共和国萨尔茨堡州的首府，是继维也纳、格拉茨和林茨之后的奥地利第四大城市。萨尔斯堡城位于奥地利西部，历史悠久、景色迷人，是音乐神童莫扎特的出生地，也是著名影片《音乐之声》的拍摄地点。其古色古香的城堡、故居、宫殿，景致迷人的街道和湖光山色，以及其他景点，都是旅客怀古、漫游的好地方。你向往电影《音乐之声》里那优美恬静的湖光山色吗？它就在奥地利的萨尔斯堡城里。

（4）Austria

奥地利。欧洲中部国家，首都维也纳，全称是 the Republic of Austria 奥地利共和国。

（5）Twinkle, Twinkle, Little Star

"小星星，亮晶晶"是一首非常流行的英语儿歌，歌词来自 19 世纪早起的一首由 Jane Taylor 写的英文诗"星星"。该诗是以对句的形式写成，于 1806 年出版在一本"儿歌集"里，由 Taylor 和她的妹妹 Ann 共同编写。歌词全文如下：

Twinkle, twinkle, little star,

How I wonder what you are!

Up above the world so high,

Like a diamond in the sky!

Repeat:

Twinkle, twinkle, little star,

How I wonder what you are! *

When the blazing sun is gone,

When he nothing shines upon,

Then you show your little light,

Twinkle, twinkle, all the night. (repeat)

Then the traveller in the dark,

Thanks you for your tiny spark,

He could not see which way to go,

If you did not twinkle so. (repeat)

In the dark blue sky you keep,

And often through my curtains peep,

For you never shut your eye,

Till the sun is in the sky. (repeat)

As your bright and tiny spark,

Lights the traveller in the dark,

Though I know not what you are,

Twinkle, twinkle, little star.

4. Notes to Module 3

Our planet is divided into many different countries which have many different races of people, different customs, and different manners. Each country has its own way of greeting people.

In the USA it is normal for men to shake hands when they meet and they are famous for death-grip handshake, but it is unusual for men to kiss when they greet each other.

The British often do no more than say "hello" when they see friends. Even adults usually shake hands only when they meet for the first time. The British do shake hands, i. e. when first introduced to new people, but they rarely shake hands when parting. In an informal situation you may see social kissing (often just a peck on the cheek), this is acceptable between men and women and also between women who know each other very well, but it is rare that you will see two British men kissing, even if it is only on the cheek.

French people, including school-children, shake hands with their friends, or kiss them on both cheeks each time they meet and they leave. That's why French people think the British are unfriendly and impolite.

In Japan it is polite and normal for men and women to bow when they greet someone.

Africans are far less structured in their greetings than Europeans. They expect a warm physical greeting, an extended handshake or a hand on the shoulder in most African cultures.

In Argentina, greetings are usually effusive with plenty of hugging and kissing, not unlike the French to kiss on both cheeks. In Argentina, men kiss women, women kiss women, but men do not kiss men.

In Islamic cultures, special care should be taken when greeting a member of the opposite sex. It is up to an Islamic woman to decide whether to offer her hand during an introduction. After all, physical contact between the sexes is limited. Never greet an Islamic woman with a kiss. You should never offer your hand to a woman first. Rather, wait to see if she offers hers to you. If she does, it is acceptable to shake it. Otherwise, a verbal greeting will suffice.

III. Language Points

■■■■■■■■■ Passage A ■■■■■■■■■

◆ Important Words ◆

performer [pə'fɔːmə] n. someone who performs in front of an audience or in public 表演者

e.g.　1. Now, Ken Kesey, some of you probably know, was a sort of performer, writer, not really an activist.

　　　2. In our art music, our symphonies, concertos genres of this sort, the performer is actually much less important.

composer [kəm'pəuzə] n. someone who writes music 作曲家

e.g.　1. This song by the Brazilian composer Antonio Carlos Jobim first became famous in the early nineteen sixties.

　　　2. Who is the composer of the piece that you're about to hear and what is its title or what's it called?

employ [ɪm'plɔɪ] vt. to have someone work or do a job for you and pay them for it 雇佣; to use sth 使用; to spend time doing sth 从事于; 忙于; 专心于

e.g.　1. The boss is going to employ Brown because he stands applicants through the interview.

　　　2. None but a wise man can employ leisure well.

　　　3. Mary has been employed in preparations for the trip all afternoon.

nobility [nəu'bɪlətɪ] n. people of high social position who have titles such as that of Duke or Duchess 贵族(阶层) [the S]; the quality of being noble in character 高贵

e.g.　1. The new rich imitated the nobility.

　　　2. He followed his principles with nobility.

brilliant ['brɪlɪənt] a. of surpassing excellence 优秀的, 杰出的; full of light; shining intensely 灿烂的, 闪耀的

e.g.　1. I mean, not only is he a brilliant scientist, but it turns out he's a Black Diamond skier.

　　　2. Her brilliant blue eyes were strongly impressed on my memory.

handicap [ˈhændɪkæp] *n.* the condition of being unable to perform as a consequence of physical or mental unfitness 残疾；*vt.* to put at a disadvantage 使不利，妨碍

e.g.　1. Blindness is a great handicap.

　　　2. Mark O'Connor is very firm that his method doesn't handicap students from playing traditional classical music.

equally [ˈiːkwəli] *ad.* to the same degree 同样地，相等地，平等地

e.g.　1. Please try to treat them equally.

　　　2. The two girls can run equally fast.

extract [ˈekstrækt] *n.* a passage selected from a larger work 摘录；提取

e.g.　1. He read several extracts from the poem.

　　　2. The article was a choice extract from her writings.

gathering [ˈgæðərɪŋ] *n.* a group of persons together in one place 聚会，集会

e.g.　1. If so, you might like to come to a gathering.

　　　2. For the first time she gave a speech before a large gathering of people.

belong [biˈlɒŋ] *vi.* to be a member of a group or organization 归属于（后接 to）

e.g.　1. What political party does he belong to?

　　　2. This cover belongs to that jar.

even though 即使

e.g.　1. He will come on time even though it rains.

　　　2. Even though you're just starting the business, you've probably done dozens of jobs for people already.

be known as 被称之为；以……著称

e.g.　1. Florida can be known as energy and green industry leaders throughout the world.

　　　2. She came to be known as a protest singer.

no longer 不再

e.g.　1. He worked and worked until he no longer hated mathematics.

　　　2. He no longer lives there.

◆ Explanation of Difficult Sentences ◆

(1) In his early twenties Beethoven moved to Vienna, where he spent the rest of his life and died on March 26, 1827.

- 贝多芬二十岁出头就迁居到维也纳,在那里度过了他的一生,死于 1827 年 3 月 26 日。
- where 引出一个表示地点的定语从句,where 指的是 Vienna 这个地方。

(2) Even though he could no longer hear well enough to play the piano, Beethoven composed some of his best music after he lost his hearing!

- 即使在弹奏钢琴时听觉不够好,他却在失去听觉之后谱写出了一些最优秀的乐谱。
- even though 用来表示一种让步的语气,well enough 表示足够好的意思。

(3) Beethoven used notebooks in which visitors could write what they wanted him to know, or equally ask what they wanted to know.

- 贝多芬采用笔记本让访问他的人写下他们想告诉贝多芬什么事情。同样,贝多芬也在笔记本上写下问他们要想知道什么。
- 本句中有一个 which 从句,两个 what 从句。in which 指代的是"在笔记本上",两个 what 从句分别表示贝多芬和来访者想知道的事情。

(4) Beethoven is considered one of the greatest musical geniuses who ever lived.

- 贝多芬被誉为过去最伟大的音乐天才之一。
- who ever lived 指的是曾经或过去的那些人。

■ Passage B ■

◆ Important Words ◆

remarkably [rɪˈmɑːkəblɪ] *ad.* unusually or strikingly 非凡地;显著地

e.g.　1. The car is in remarkably good condition for its age.

　　　2. Remarkably, nobody was injured.

intense [ɪnˈtens] *a.* (of a person) having or showing very strong feelings, opinions or thoughts about sb/sth 热情的;very great; very strong 极度的

e.g.　1. He's very intense about everything.

　　　2. He is under intense pressure to resign.

minor [ˈmaɪnə(r)] *a.* of lesser importance or stature or rank 不重要的

e.g.　1. Stress may result in minor illness.

　　　2. If penicillin had not been available, many people would have died from bacterial illnesses or even minor wounds.

7

fascination[ˌfæsɪˈneɪʃn]*n.* the state of being intensely interested; the capacity to attract intense interest 入神;迷恋

e. g.　1. A little boy had a fascination for motorcycles.

　　　　2. I was too little to reach the telephone, but used to listen with fascination when my mother talked to it.

fault[fɔːlt]*n.* responsibility for a bad situation or event 错误

e. g.　1. Why are you always finding fault?

　　　　2. It's really my fault for being careless.

eventually[ɪˈventʃuəlɪ]*ad.* after a long period of time or an especially long delay 最后

e. g.　1. The current economic environment will eventually improve.

　　　　2. Eventually I decided to take this opportunity.

impressive[ɪmˈpresɪv]*a.* making a strong or vivid impression 给人留下深刻印象的

e. g.　1. This is the most impressive architecture I've seen on this trip.

　　　　2. At first glance, all this has produced some impressive results.

evident[ˈevɪdənt]*a.* clearly revealed to the mind or the senses or judgment, or capable of being seen or noticed 明显的

e. g.　1. It's evident that you are tired.

　　　　2. That China does matter is evident from its impact on the global economy.

twinkle[ˈtwɪŋkl]*vi.* to emit or reflect light in a flickering manner 闪烁

e. g.　1. Stars twinkled in the night sky.

　　　　2. Her eyes twinkled when she heard the news.

portray[pɔːˈtreɪ]*vt.* to describe or show sb/sth in a particular way in a painting, drawing, sculpture, etc. 描绘;to act a particular role in a film/movie or play 扮演

e. g.　1. The father is portrayed as a good-looking man in this painting.

　　　　2. It is still considered improper to portray Christ in a play or film.

except for 除……之外,除了

e. g.　1. An instrument made by an old master can now be copied in every detail—except for the sound.

　　　　2. The region is uninhabited except for a few scattered mountain villages.

give up 放弃

e. g.   1. We will not give up until we find convincing evidence.

2. No. I mean, do you think I should give up drawing and go into business with my father?

end up 以……结束,以……告终

e. g.   1. How does the film end up?

2. They took the wrong train and ended up at a small station.

far from 完全不,远远不

e. g.   1. His work is far from satisfactory.

2. He is not handsome, far from it.

◆ Explanation of Difficult Sentences ◆

(1) Wolfgang Amadeus Mozart was born in 1756 in what is now Salzburg, Austria, …

- 沃尔夫冈·阿马德乌斯·莫扎特1756年出生在当今奥地利的萨尔斯堡。
- "what is now…"作为介词 in 的宾语,表示现在这个地名的名称。

(2) One person described Mozart as "a remarkably small man, very thin and pale, and there is nothing special about him, giving no signs of his genius except for his large intense eyes."

- 据描述,莫扎特的个头相当矮小,人也瘦,且一副苍白的面孔,看不出有一点特别的,也没有丁点天才的迹象,但他有一双炯炯有神的大眼。
- very thin and pale 是形容词,表示伴随状态,用于补充说明。"giving no signs of…"是分词短语,起到进一步解释的作用。

(3) When Mozart's sister was seven she began keyboard lessons with her father while the three-year-old Mozart watched with fascination.

- 莫扎特的姐姐7岁时就跟其父亲学练弹琴,而3岁的莫扎特总会在一旁聚精会神地观看。
- 本句由连词 while 连接两个单句,表示"在同时",通常用于对照。

(4) But far from being hard up, Mozart lived a rich life and was among the top earners in eighteenth century Vienna.

- 其实莫扎特根本说不上缺钱,他过得很富裕,曾是18世纪维也纳挣钱最多的人之一。
- far from 为固定词组,意为"完全不,远远不";hard up 意为"缺钱的,手头紧的";"be among…"等同于"one of…",意为"……之一"。

IV. Keys, Tapescripts and Text Translations

━━ Keys ━━

◆ Lead-in ◆

1. 土耳其进行曲
2. Open.

◆ Module 1　Learn to Talk ◆

Meeting New Friends

1. *John and Mary meet each other for the first time on campus. Listen to the model dialogue, and underline the expressions of greetings and introductions.*

   John：<u>Hi! I'm</u> John Smith.

   Mary：<u>How do you do</u>, Mr. Smith. <u>My name is</u> Mary Brown.

   John：But <u>you can call me</u> Johnnie. Can I call you Mary, Miss Brown.

   Mary：Yes, please. <u>It's nice to meet you</u>, Johnnie.

   John：<u>Nice to meet you, too.</u>

   Mary：I'm a freshman here. <u>What about you,</u> Johnnie?

   John：<u>Me, too.</u> I study music in the Academy of Arts at Chongqing University.

   Mary：That's interesting.

   John：<u>What do you do,</u> Mary?

   Mary：I'm a student in Meishi Film Academy.

   John：We are probably going to be in the same English class.

   Mary：<u>That would be great!</u>

2. Open.

3. *Listen to the conversation among James, Wang Dong and Cathy from an English class. Fill in the names of the speakers with the following pictures.*

   a. Wang Dong likes reading comic books.

   b. Cathy enjoys going to a yoga class.

   c. James likes playing football.

4. *Listen again and decide whether the following statements are true (T) or false (F).*

   (1)F　(2)T　(3)T　(4)F　(5)T　(6)F

5. Open.　6. Open.

Stories of Musicians

Before You Listen

1. Open.　2. Open.

While You Listen

1. *Listen and answer the questions about Bach and Chopin. Check (√) the correct box.*

Who...	Bach	Chopin
(1) was born in Germany?	√	□
(2) was Polish?	□	√
(3) was brought up by his older brother?	√	□
(4) gave his first concert at the age of eight?	□	√
(5) never went back to his motherland?	□	√
(6) held three major jobs in his life?	√	□
(7) wrote all kinds of music for organ and other keyboard instruments?	√	□
(8) died at the age of 39?	□	√

2. *Listen again and fill in the following table about the influence of family on Bach and Chopin.*

	Family influence
Bach	(1) His father was a <u>town musician.</u> (2) He came from a long line of <u>composers</u> – over 300 years' worth of Bachs all worked as <u>professional musicians.</u> (3) His older brother was a <u>church</u> organist.
Chopin	His mother introduced him to the <u>piano.</u>

After You Listen

Open.

◆ Module 2　Learn to Read ◆

Warm-up

Open.

Passage A　Life of Beethoven

Reading Comprehension

1. *Global understanding*

　(1) The passage mainly introduces Beethoven's early life and how he composed his best music after he lost his hearing.

　(2) The author thinks that Beethoven is a musical genius.

(3) The author quotes an extract from Beethoven's letter to show that Beethoven wrote many kinds of music under great pressure when he became a deaf.

2. *Detailed understanding*

(1) B (2) B (3) C (4) D (5) C

Language Practice

1. Open.

2. *Identify the words or expressions which mark or indicate the time periods. Then think of a similar word or expression which could replace each of them.*

Words or expressions indicating the time periods	Similar words or expressions
after a while	soon after; before long; after a short time; a little while
soon	quickly; in a short time
in his early twenties	soon after he was twenties
when he was around 30 years old	about his thirties; at about age 30; at the age of 30 or so
the rest of his life	the remainder of one's life; one's remaining years

3. *Translate the following sentences, paying special attention to the coloured parts.*

(1) A. 学校的自助餐厅雇佣了一些学生当临时工。

   B. 她利用所有的业余时间听古典音乐。

(2) A. 我们读了一些 19 世纪的小说摘录。

   B. 各种颜色的染料均可从植物中提取。

(3) A. 耀眼的阳光使得她不停地眨眼。

   B. 他在大学读书时曾是一位才华横溢的学生。

(4) 贝多芬用笔记本让来访的人把他们想要告诉给他的事情写上去。

(5) 贝多芬二十出头就搬到维也纳居住,他在那里度过了余生,死于 1827 年 3 月 26 日。

Passage B   Musical Genius: Mozart

Reading Comprehension

1. *Global understanding*

Paragraph 1: c   Paragraph 2: a   Paragraph 3: b

2. *Detailed understanding*

(1) A (2) D (3) B (4) C

3. *Information scanning*

Time	Things that happened to Mozart
At age 4	(1) He began keyboard lessons playing without fault.
(2) By age 5	He was composing short pieces of music.
(3) At age 6	He began traveling through Europe with his sister and father.
While touring in Europe	(4) Mozart learned to play the violin and the organ.
At age 8	He published his first two sonatas.
At age 13	(5) He composed his first opera.
(6) At age 4 or 5	It is said that he composed the tune to "Twinkle, Twinkle, Little Star".
(7) In 1791	He died in Vienna.

Language Practice

1. *Make sure you know the words in the table below. Choose the correct word or phrase to complete each of the following sentences. Change form where necessary.*

　　(1) at the request of　(2) fascinations　(3) impressive　(4) talents　(5) portrayed

2. *Complete the following sentences by translating into English the Chinese given in brackets.*

　　(1) live a very comfortable life

　　(2) while he is listening with fascination

　　(3) At age three/At the age of three/When he was three years old

　　(4) Far from being poor

　　(5) what used to be a wild

◆Module 3　Culture Link◆

Quiz

1. c　American people　　　　　2. b　British people

3. a　French people　　　　　　4. h　Japanese people

5. g　Most African people　　　　6. f　Argentines

7. e　People in Islamic cultures　　8. d　Thai people

◆Module 4　Scenario Link◆

Open.

■■■■■ Tapescripts ■■■■■

◆Module 1　Learn to Talk◆

Meeting New Friends

3. *Listen to the conversation among James, Wang Dong and Cathy from an English class. Fill in the names of the speakers with the following pictures.*

James：　　Hi, my name is James Smith. I'm from Britain. I'm 18, and I study Chinese painting in Academy of Arts. In my free time, I like sailing and playing football.

Cathy: Hi, I'm Cathy. I'm from Brazil. I'm 28 and I'm married. I have one child. I'm also a student, like James. I have come to China to study music. When I'm not studying, I like going to a yoga class.

Wang Dong: Hi, I am called Wang Dong and I am from China. I'm 19 and I study graphic arts. When I have some free time, I like reading books.

Stories of Musicians

Johann Sebastian Bach was born in Eisenach, Germany, where his father was a town musician. Bach came from a long line of composers—over 300 years' worth of Bachs all worked as professional musicians. By the time Johann was 10, both his parents had died, so he was brought up by his older brother, who was a church organist. Johann became a very good organist, too.

Johann Sebastian Bach held three major jobs in his life: First he worked for a duke, then for a prince, and finally, he became director of music at the St. Thomas Church and School in Leipzig, Germany. Even though his job in Leipzig kept him very busy in his spare time, Bach conducted a group of musicians who liked to get together to perform at a local coffee house.

During his lifetime, people thought of Bach as just an ordinary working musician. No one really knew much about his music until 100 years after his death, when another composer, Felix Mendelssohn, conducted a performance of Bach's St. Matthew Passion.

Bach is now seen as one of the greatest geniuses in music history. He wrote all kinds of music for organ and other keyboard instruments, orchestras, choirs, and concertos for many different instrumental combinations.

Frédéric Chopin was one of the greatest pianists of his day. Chopin was born in a town just outside of Warsaw, Poland. His mother introduced him to the piano; by the time he was six, Chopin played extremely well and was starting to compose. He gave his first concert at the age of eight.

When Chopin was 20, he left Poland to seek fame and fortune in other European cities. When Chopin got to Paris, he decided to stay.

There's a story that when Chopin left his native country, his friends gave him some Polish soil, which he carried around with him for the rest of his life. That's probably not true, but Chopin did continue to be passionately patriotic about Poland, even though he never went back there.

Chopin was never healthy, and he was only thirty-nine when he died of tuberculosis. When he was buried in France—a special box of earth was brought from Poland to sprinkle on his grave. But Chopin's heart is in Poland-literally. His heart was put in an urn and taken to the Church of the Holy Cross in Warsaw.

◆ Module 2　Learn to Read ◆

Warm-up（**Passage A**）

Good morning, class. Today we are going to talk about Beethoven and Alechikis. These song writers are very inspirational in their songs and everyday life.

Let's start with Beethoven. Can anyone tell me what they already know about Beethoven? Anyone? Okay then, I will start to talk him.

Beethoven's full name is Ludwig van Beethoven, and his nationality is German.

Beethoven's date of birth year is 1770, and he died in 1827. His career title was a composer. To describe his life, he had a abusive father which was alcolholic. Beethoven's father was also abusive to him in a physical, mental, ribald and emotional way. Beethoven was really close to his mother. One time Beethoven's father lied about his age during a concert so people could reckon him on. His father also took advantage of his talent. Some of his famous works as *Moon Lights* and other, and furtherness, symphony, are no doubtly joyful. Joyfully adoreded, his contributions were that he wanted to change the face of music, and his story is very inspirational once again. This death was the end of an era. He raised a bar from musicians. That's all for today's class. Get ready for Alechikis tomorrow.

■ Text Translations ■

◆ Passage A ◆

贝多芬的一生

　　路德维希·范·贝多芬 1770 年 12 月 16 日生于德国的波恩,其父曾是一名歌手,是贝多芬的启蒙老师。不久以后,即使贝多芬还是一个小孩,他却常常参加巡演,以此来支持家庭。贝多芬在二十岁出头就迁居到维也纳,在那里度过了一生,于 1827 年 3 月 26 日与世长辞。

　　贝多芬是靠谱曲来维持生活的作曲家之一,没有受雇于教堂或是贵族。开始他是以才气横溢的钢琴手而出名,但到了 30 岁左右时贝多芬逐渐失去了听觉。即使在弹奏钢琴时听觉不好,他却在失去听觉之后谱写了一些最优秀的乐谱。

　　在他再也隐瞒不住其听觉障碍后,贝多芬采用笔记本让访问他的人写下他们想告诉贝多芬什么事情,同样,贝多芬也在笔记本上写下问他们要想知道什么。

　　下面是一段摘录,是贝多芬写给友人的信:

　　"……两年以来我一直躲避几乎所有的社交活动,要让我对别人说'我是一个聋子',这是完全不可能的。假若我干的是其他职业,这还较容易,但对我的职业来说,这太可怕了。"

　　贝多芬被誉为过去最伟大的音乐天才之一。也许让他最有名气的是他的九部交响乐。他也谱写了其他类型的音乐,如:室内音乐、圣咏曲、钢琴曲、弦乐四重奏曲,以及一部歌剧。

◆ Passage B ◆

音乐天才:莫扎特

　　沃尔夫冈·阿马德乌斯·莫扎特 1756 年出生在当今奥地利的萨尔斯堡,于 1791 年死于维也纳。据描述,莫扎特的个头相当矮小,人也瘦,且一副苍白的面孔,看不出有一点特别的,也没有丁点天才的迹象,但他有一双炯炯有神的大眼。

　　莫扎特的父亲是一位名不见经传的作曲者,但却是一位经验丰富的老师。莫扎特的姐姐7岁时就跟其父亲学练弹琴,而3岁的莫扎特总会在一旁聚精会神地观看。4岁时,莫扎特自己开始上钢琴课,弹奏得非常精准,而且乐感也很强。5岁时莫扎特就能作曲,父亲为他将这些曲子写下来。当年轻的莫扎特的音乐天赋日益明显时,最后,他父亲决定放弃作曲。莫扎特6岁时便和她的姐姐跟着他们的父亲开始周游欧洲,在那些宫廷里举办音乐会。在巡演中,莫扎特学会了拉小提琴和演奏管风琴。莫扎特8岁时首次发布了两部奏鸣曲,用拨弦古钢琴演奏。13岁时,莫扎特应一位君主要求谱写了他的第一部歌剧。不少人认为,"小星星,亮晶晶"这首儿歌的曲子就是莫扎特谱写的,当时他只有4岁或是5岁。

　　几百年以来,人们一直认为莫扎特是一位贫穷的天才,他曾向伙伴们写过求助信,他最终也葬于贫民的坟墓。其实莫扎特根本说不上缺钱,他过得很富裕,也曾是18世纪维也纳挣钱最多的人之一。

Unit 2　Painters

I. Background Information

Painting is the practice of applying paint, pigment, color or other medium to a surface (support base). The application of the medium is commonly applied to the base with a brush but other objects can be used. Paintings may have for their support such surfaces as walls, paper, canvas, wood, glass, lacquer, clay, copper or concrete, and so on.

Painting is a mode of expression and the forms are numerous. Drawing, composition or abstraction and other aesthetics may serve to manifest the expressive and conceptual intention of the practitioner. Paintings can be naturalistic, representational (as in a still life or landscape painting), photographic, abstract, and can be loaded with narrative content, symbolism, emotion or be political in nature.

In the west, there are some painting styles: Realism, Baroque, Rococo, Expressionism, Impressionism, Modernism, Cubism, Pop art, and so on. Here styles can refer to the distinctive visual elements, techniques and methods that typify an individual artist's work. It can also refer to the movement or school that an artist is associated with.

How to become a painter:

We all have the desire to paint. However, we feel that we have to be "perfect" like Van Gogh, but this is far from the truth. All you need is paint, a paint brush, a piece of paper, and your imagination.

First you want to figure out what type of paint you want to work with. There are several paints to choose from: oil, acrylic, finger paint, and water colored pencils. You will need paint brushes as there are specific paint brushes for the type of paint you are going to work with. Choose a canvas or a sketch pad to paint with. Sketch pads are good to use at first to practice.

Decide on a design you would like to work with. Practice the designs in the sketch pad. Don't worry if you mess up, this is only practice. Use your imagination. Make circles, sway the brush back and forth, dab the brush making splash images, and have fun. There is no wrong or right way of painting, sometimes our silliest mistakes become our masterpieces. For a little inspiration, try painting outside or by a window, listening to music, and lighting candles.

II. Notes

1. Notes to Lead-in

The Starring Sky《星空》:这是一幅既亲近又茫远的风景画,高大的白扬树战栗着悠然地浮现在我们

面前;山谷里的小村庄,在尖顶教堂的保护之下安然栖息;宇宙里所有的恒星和行星在"最后的审判"中旋转着、爆发着。这不是对人,而是对太阳系的最后审判。这件作品是梵·高在圣雷米疗养院画的,时间是1889年6月。梵·高的神经第二次崩溃之后,就住进了这座疗养院。在那儿,他的病情时好时坏,在神志清醒而充满了情感的时候,他就不停地画画。色彩主要是蓝和紫罗兰,同时有规律地跳动着星星发光的黄色。前景中深绿和棕色的白杨树,意味着包围了这个世界的茫茫之夜。记得一句关于梵·高的话:"灿烂到极致不是黯淡就是死亡,所以梵·高也只能,毁灭了自己。"

2. Notes to Module 1

(1) Mogan Museum

摩根博物馆坐落于曼哈顿中城的东36街与麦迪逊大道交会处,收藏了从古代到中世纪,文艺复兴时期到当代的艺术、文学和音乐作品,是世界上最好的博物馆之一。

(2) Leonardo da Vinci

列奥纳多·达·芬奇(1452年4月15日—1519年5月2日),是一位意大利文艺复兴时期的多项领域博学者,其同时是建筑师、解剖学者、艺术家、工程师、数学家、发明家。他无穷的好奇与创意使得他成为文艺复兴时期典型的艺术家,而且也是历史上最著名的画家之一。他与米开朗基罗和拉斐尔并称"文艺复兴三杰"。

(3) The Renaissance

文艺复兴时期始于14世纪初,结束于16世纪初。它的本意即"重生"或"重建"。在这段时间里,人文精神得以重生,各种艺术形式也开始复活。艺术家的作品展现了更多的艺术自由和个人主义。这种创造力使艺术家摈弃了中世纪的严格方式。他们的艺术重现了古希腊的理想。

(4) the Museum of Louvre

卢浮宫是世界上最古老、最大、最著名的博物馆之一,位于法国巴黎市中心的塞纳河北岸(右岸),始建于1204年,历经800多年扩建、重修达到今天的规模。它的整体建筑呈"U"形,分为新、老两部分,老的建于路易十四时期,新的建于拿破仑时代。宫前的金字塔形玻璃入口,是华人建筑大师贝聿铭设计的。同时,卢浮宫也是法国历史上最悠久的王宫。藏品中有被誉为世界三宝的《维纳斯》雕像、《蒙娜丽莎》油画和《胜利女神》石雕,更有大量希腊、罗马、埃及及东方的古董。

(5) Michelangelo Buonarroti

米开朗基罗·博那罗蒂(1475—1564),意大利文艺复兴时期伟大的绘画家、雕塑家、建筑师和诗人,文艺复兴时期雕塑艺术最高峰的代表。与拉斐尔和达芬奇并称为"文艺复兴三杰"。代表作品有《大卫》《摩西》《奴隶》《创世纪》等。

3. Notes to Module 2

(1) Pablo Picasso

帕巴洛·毕加索(1881—1973)是西班牙人,自幼有非凡的艺术才能。他是现代艺术(立体派)的创始人,西方现代派绘画的主要代表。毕加索是个不断变化艺术手法的探求者。印象派、后期印象派、野兽的艺术手法都被他汲取改造为自己的风格。他的才能在于,他的各种变异风格中,都保持自己粗犷刚劲的个性,而且在各种手法的使用中,都能达到内部的统一与和谐。

（2）Georges Braque

　　乔治·勃拉克(1882—1963)，法国画家，立体主义代表。1882 年 5 月 13 日生于塞纳河畔的阿让特伊，1963 年 8 月 31 日卒于巴黎。他的影响实际上并不比毕加索小。他与毕加索同为立体主义运动的创始者，并且"立体主义"这一名称还是由他的作品而来。

（3）the Blue Period

　　蓝色时期：毕加索早期创作的一段时期。毕加索当时的生活条件很差，又受到德加、雅西尔与土鲁斯·劳特累克画风的影响，加上在西班牙受教育时染上的西班牙式的忧伤主义，这时期的作品弥漫着一片阴沉的蓝郁。

（4）Cubism

　　立体主义是前卫艺术运动的一个流派，对 20 世纪初期的欧洲绘画与雕塑带来革命。

　　立体主义的艺术家追求碎裂、解析、重新组合的形式，形成分离的画面——以许多组合的碎片形态为艺术家们所要展现的目标。艺术家从许多的角度来描写对象物，将其置于同一个画面之中，以此来表达对象物最为完整的形象。

（5）*Guernica*

　　《格尔尼卡》，毕加索的名画之一，立体派的代表作。1937 年 4 月 26 日，发生了德国空军轰炸西班牙北部巴克斯重镇格尔尼卡的事件。德军 3 个小时的轰炸，炸死炸伤了很多平民百姓，使格尔尼卡化为平地。德军的这一罪行激起了国际舆论的谴责。毕加索义愤填膺，决定就以这一事件作为壁画创作的题材，以表达自己对战争罪犯的抗议和对这次事件中死去的人的哀悼。这幅画运用立体主义的绘画形式，以变形、象征和寓意的手法描绘了在法西斯兽行下，人民惊恐、痛苦和死亡的悲惨情景。

（6）the Dutch Reformed Church

　　荷兰改革教会，荷兰最大的基督教会，其前身是 16 世纪宗教改革运动时期成立的荷兰国家教会。

III. Language Points

■■■■ Passage A ■■■■

◆ Important Words ◆

depiction[dɪˈpɪkʃn]*n.* a picture that shows an image of sb/sth 描述

　　e.g.　1. Madonna in Christian art, is a depiction of the Virgin Mary.

　　　　　2. Is the model an accurate depiction of the program?

prolific[prəˈlɪfɪk]*a.* producing works, or fruit in great abundance 多产的；丰富的

　　e.g.　1. He was a great entertainer, a deep thinker, a prolific author and composer.

　　　　　2. We do not know that even the most prolific area is fully stocked with specific forms.

deem[diːm]*vt.* to regard as; consider 认定

　　e.g.　1. Do you deem this plan sensible?

　　　　　2. I deem it my duty to help the poor.

sculpture[ˈskʌlptʃə(r)]*n*. a work of art that is a solid figure or object made by carving or shaping wood, stone, metal, clay, etc. 雕塑品;雕像

e. g.　1. We saw sculptures of ancient Roman gods.

　　　2. He was known for his sculpture of The Fates.

canvas[ˈkænvəs]*n*. a piece of such fabric on which a painting, especially an oil painting, is executed(帆布)画布

e. g.　1. The vase became his canvas.

　　　2. Life is a great big canvas, and you should throw all the paint on it as you can.

embody[ɪmˈbɒdɪ]*vt*. to represent in bodily or material form 体现

e. g.　1. As the middle school student, what respect does patriotism spirit embody in?

　　　2. The new model of car embodies many improvements.

distinguished[dɪˈstɪŋgwɪʃt]*a*. characterized by excellence or distinction 杰出的;著名的

e. g.　1. The Chinese nation is distinguished for its diligence and courage.

　　　2. He was very popular, a distinguished fashion figure as well as financier.

restore[rɪˈstɔː(r)]*vt*. to bring back into existence or use; reestablish 恢复;修复;归还

e. g.　1. He also promises to restore trust in government.

　　　2. The old temple was restored during the early nineteenth century.

democracy[dɪˈmɒkrəsɪ]*n*. the common people, considered as the primary source of political power 民主;民主主义;民主政治

e. g.　1. socialist democracy

　　　2. A true democracy allows free speech.

along with 和……一起;除……以外(还)

e. g.　1. All we need is some creativity along with plenty of time and practice.

　　　2. Early in December the foreman came along with generous food for Christmas.

a body of 大量

e. g.　1. A body of soliders attacked Mr. Moore's shop last night.

　　　2. He has read a body of foreign novels.

◆ Explanation of Difficult Sentences ◆

(1) Pablo Picasso, a Spanish painter, was one of the recognized masters of 20th century art, probably most famous as the founder, along with Georges Braque, of Cubism.

- 西班牙画家帕巴洛·毕加索(1881—1973)是 20 世纪公认的艺术大师之一,也因和乔治·勃拉克一起成立了立体主义画派而蜚声海内外。
- Pablo Picasso was one of the art masters who are admired and accepted by most of the people in 20th century. He became very famous because he and Georges Braque founded Cubism together.

(2) However, over his long life he produced a wide and varied body of work, the best known being the Blue Period works which feature moving depictions of acrobats, beggars, and artists.

- 在他漫长的一生中,他创作了广泛和变化多样的作品。其中最著名的是蓝色时期的作品,描绘了杂技演员,乞丐和艺术家的各种姿态。
- During his whole life, he made a large number and kinds of work. The Blue Period works are the most famous, which show us the real lives of acrobats, beggars and artists.

(3) Picasso was the most prolific painter ever, as deemed in the *Guinness Book of Records*.

- 毕加索也是《吉尼斯世界纪录大全》里承认的最多产的画家。
- According to the *Guinness Book of Records*, the number of Picasso's works was the largest in the world.

(4) Picasso's most famous work is his depiction of the German bombing of Guernica, Spain, titled *Guernica*. For many people, this large canvas embodies the inhumanity and hopelessness of war.

- 毕加索最著名的作品是描述德国轰炸西班牙小镇格尔尼卡的一幅油画:《格尔尼卡》。这幅大型油画向众人展现了战争的非人道和绝望。
- In his most famous work: *Guernica*, Picasso described the German bombing of Guernica, Spain. The large oil painting shows us people's pains brought by war and the cruelty of war.

(5) The act of painting was captured in a series of photographs by Picasso's most famous lover, Dora Maar, a distinguished artist in her own right.

- 毕加索最著名的爱人,本身也是一位杰出艺术家的多洛·玛尔用一系列照片记录了油画的创作过程。
- Dora Maar, Picasso's most famous lover, who herself was a very excellent artist, recorded Picasso's producing process of Guernica by taking many pictures.

(6) Picasso promised that the painting should not return to Spain until democracy was restored in that country.

- 毕加索承诺,只有西班牙重建民主后,这幅画才能送回西班牙。

21

• Picasso promised that only when Spain became a democratic country again, should the painting return to the country.

▰ **Passage B** ▰

◆ Important Words ◆

occupation[ˌɒkjuˈpeɪʃn]*n.* a vocation; the act or process of holding or possessing a place 职业；占有

e.g.　1. Why did you choose the occupation of a secretary?

　　　2. The Nazi occupation met with little resistance.

gravitate[ˈɡrævɪteɪt]*vi.* to be attracted by or as if by an irresistible force 受吸引|

e.g.　1. Let your soul gravitate to the love!

　　　2. In summer people gravitate to the seaside.

far-reaching[fɑː-ˈriːtʃɪŋ]*a.* having a wide range, influence, or effect 意义深远的

e.g.　1. Some observers believe change will be far-reaching.

　　　2. This military training has a far-reaching influence on the boy.

impact[ˈɪmpækt]*n.* the effect or impression of one thing on another 影响；撞击；冲突

e.g.　1. Some people these days suggest we all drive less to reduce the impact of climate change.

　　　2. How will the war impact on his generation?

bout[baʊt]*n.* an attack or period of illness; a period of time spent in a particular way; a spell 发作；一阵

e.g.　1. He had a long bout of illness last year.

　　　2. It may be too late to avoid another bout of price rises.

self-inflicted[self-ɪnˈflɪktɪd]*a.* inflicted or imposed on oneself 自我造成的

e.g.　1. Stress from this kind of jealousy is self-inflicted.

　　　2. All of these are self-inflicted to some extent — do they annoy you too?

contributor[kənˈtrɪbjətə(r)]*n.* a person or thing that provides money to help pay for sth, or support sth 贡献者；捐助者

e.g.　1. Migrant workers are important contributors to the city construction.

　　　2. a generous contributor to charity.

the same... as 与……一样

e. g.　1. George doesn't look the same as before.

　　　　2. But economic power is not the same as political power.

throughout one's life 整个一生

e. g.　1. There are not many opportunities throughout one's life.

　　　　2. Life long education means a sustainable study after one's graduation from a university throughout one's life.

during this time 在此期间

e. g.　1. Some teachers give us quizes during this time.

　　　　2. Would you like to have been in school during this time period?

suffer from 遭受,忍受(痛苦、磨难)

e. g.　1. Some children suffer from measles.

　　　　2. Professor O says some people suffer from midlife depression more than others.

regard as 当作

e. g.　1. "Titanic" is regarded as his best film so far.

　　　　2. What my friends consider to be modern, I often regard as ugly.

◆ Explanation of Difficult Sentences ◆

(1)... his grandfather, Vincent (1789 – 1874), had received his degree of theology at the University of Leiden in 1811. ... So art and religion were the two occupations to which the Van Gogh family gravitated.

- 他的祖父温森特于1811年在雷登大学获得神学学位。……所以艺术和宗教是梵·高家族喜爱的两个职业。

- His grandfather graduated from the University of Leiden in 1811, with a degree of theology... Therefore, the members of Van Gogh family were used to choosing art or religion as their professions.

(2) His works grew brighter in colour and he developed the unique and highly recognizable style which became fully realized during his stay in Arles in 1888.

- 他的作品在色彩上日趋明亮,形成了独特并受到高度认可的风格。1888年,当他待在阿尔镇时,这种风格完全成熟。

- The colors of his work became briighter and brighter and Van Gogh developed his own special and well known style, which was then formed completely in Arles.

23

（3）Van Gogh's work had a far-reaching influence on 20th century art because of its vivid colours and emotional impact.

- 梵·高的作品色彩生动,情感丰沛,对 20 世纪的艺术产生了深远影响。
- The work of Van Gogh had bright colors and strong feeling, which got a long-term influence on the art of 20th century .

（4）He suffered from anxiety and increasingly frequent bouts of mental illness throughout his life, and died… from a self-inflicted gunshot wound.

- 但是他深受焦虑和日益频繁发作的精神疾病困扰,因此……他开枪自杀,悄然离世。
- He always felt anxious and his mental illness became more and more serious… finally he hurt himself with a gun and died from the serious wound.

IV. Keys, Tapescripts and Text Translations

■ Keys ■

◆Lead-in◆

1. 星空(Starry Night)
2. Open.

◆Module 1　Learn to Talk◆

Describing Places and Objects

1. *Sandra is telling Mike about a painting. Listen to the model dialogue, and underline the expressions of describing objects.*

Sandra：Mike, I'm so excited! I just bought a very wonderful painting last week.

Mike：Really? Tell me about it.

Sandra：Well, it cost me 80,000 dollars.

Mike：What? 80,000 dollars? It's too expensive. But how do you like it?

Sandra：It looks very nice. It is an extremely beautiful landscape painting.

Mike：What about the size?

Sandra：Well, it's very small.

Mike：How about the color?

Sandra：Oh, it's colorful. I love the color, especially the blue.

Mike：Good, where is it?

Sandra：It's on the wall in my living room.

Mike：Can I appreciate it someday?

Sandra：Sure.

Mike：Thank you very much.

2. Open.

3. *Listen to a conversation carefully and decide whether the following statements are true (T) or false (F).*

(1) T　(2) T　(3) F　(4) F　(5) F

4. *Listen to the conversation again, and fill in the blanks with the missing words.*

(1) exhibition　(2) block　(3) find　(4) see, painting, wonderful

5. Open.

Stories of Musicians

Before You Listen

1. Open.　2. Open.

While You Listen

1. *Listen and answer the questions about Da Vinci and Raphael. Check (√) the correct box.*

Who…	Da Vinci	Raphael
(1) was a scientist and engineer?	√	☐
(2) was given the early training by his father?	☐	√
(3) was called "the prince of painters"?	☐	√
(4) became a master at 17?	☐	√
(5) spent his final years in France?	√	☐
(6) produced *the Last Supper*?	√	☐
(7) draw numerous Madonnas?	☐	√
(8) died on his 37th birthday?	☐	√

2. *Listen again and fill in the following table about the paintings by Da Vinci and Raphael.*

	Paintings
Da Vinci	(1) *The Mona Lisa* is an amazing portrait painting. (2) *The Last Supper* shows a scene of Jesus Christ during his final days.
Raphael	The sweet charm and grace of Raphael's Madonnas have got the world's love.

After You Listen

Open.

◆ Module 2　Learn to Read ◆

Warm-up

Open.

Passage A　The Most Prolific Painter–Pablo Picasso

Reading Comprehension

1. *Global understanding*

   (1) This passage mainly introduces Picasso's work, especially the painting *Guernica*.

   (2) The author thinks he is one of the recognized masters of 20th century art.

   (3) Picasso hated wars because his paintings embodied the inhumanity and hopelessness of wars.

2. *Detailed understanding*

   (1) D　(2) D　(3) C　(4) B　(5) A

Language Practice

1. *Make sure you know the words in the table below. Choose the word or phrase to complete each of the following sentences. Change the form where necessary.*

   (1) deemed　(2) prolific　(3) along with　(4) restore　(5) embodies

2. *Write a sentence by using each of the following phrases on the underlined space.*

   (1) along with

   Yesterday I played basketball along with my classmates.

   (2) a body of

   The officers had a growing body of evidence to prove him of the crime.

   (3) a series of

   The peasants got a series of good harvests.

   (4) in one's own right

   Elizabeth Ⅱ is queen of England in her own right.

3. *Translate the following sentences into Chinese, paying special attention to the coloured parts.*

   (1) 毕加索是 20 世纪公认的艺术大师,并因和乔治·勃拉克一起创建了立体派而闻名于世。

   (2) 毕加索是《吉尼斯世界纪录大全》所认定的最多产的画家。

   (3) 截至 1973 年,毕加索所有作品的价值估计为 7 亿 5 千万。

   (4) 这幅大型油画作品展现了战争的非人道和给人们带来的绝望。

   (5) 毕加索保证,如果西班牙没有恢复民主,这幅作品就不会被带回该国。

Passage B　Van Gogh

Reading Comprehension

1. *Global understanding*

   Paragraph 1：b　Paragraph 2：c　Paragraph 3：a

2. *Detailed understanding*

   (1)B　(2)A　(3)A　(4)D

3. *Information scanning*

Time	Things that happened to Mozart
In March 1853	(1) Vincent Van Gogh was born.
(2) During his early adulthood	He worked for a firm of art dealers.
(3) From 1879	He worked as a missionary in a mining region.
(4) In March 1886	He discovered the French Impressionists.
In 1888	(5) he developed the unique and highly recognizable style.
At the age of 37	(6) He shot himself with a gun.

Language Practice

1. *Make sure you know the words in the table below. Choose the word or phrase to complete each of the following sentences. Change the form where necessary.*

   (1) gravitate　(2) impact　(3) far-reaching　(4) suffered from　(5) contributor

2. *Complete the following sentences by translating into English the Chinese given in brackets.*

   (1) he has the same appearance as Jim.

   (2) she gravitates to the scene here.

   (3) throughout his life.

   (4) he often suffers from toothache.

   (5) regard him as a movie star.

◆Module 3　Culture Link◆

What Do Americans Drink?

The majority of Americans drink some types of beverages while eating. After eating some may drink a variety of things：soda, beer, wine or some kind of juice. Some people drink coffee, some people drink dessert wine, some people drink black-tea, it depends on what native they are!

If Americans have a formal meal in the morning, the breakfast is almost always accompanied by coffee and tea, often also by milk, orange juice, and less often grapefruit or tomato juice. There are some alcoholic breakfast drinks that are consumed on special occasions (or more often if there's a drinking problem)：mimosa (含羞草) (equal parts orange juice and champagne) and bloody Mary

（血腥玛丽）（vodka 伏特加）or gin, tomato juice, optional hot pepper sauce, over ice with a stalk of celery as a garnish）.

Office workers in America usually start work at nine or earlier. At about eleven o'clock they have a short break, known as the coffee break during which they drink coffee or tea and have some refreshment. Coffee is provided free. At about four clock in the afternoon, another coffee break is given.

At the noon or evening meal, a formal approach would include pre-dinner alcoholic drinks-which could be any variety of cocktail, wine or beer or non-alcoholic sodas in some cases. The meal itself, in most formal settings, will include wine (which is supposed to be chosen by the host to match well with the flavors of the food) and water. The conclusion of the meal will include coffee or tea, and the more common after-dinner alcoholic drinks would include flavourful liqueurs like Amaretto, Sambuca, Kahlua, etc. but just about any cocktail, beer, or wine could be served after dinner as well.

Again, that's just the formal pattern. There are many lower-class Americans who pop a can of beer open upon awakening and continue to consume one or more cans per hour all day long. Another wide segment of Americans will never consume alcohol. The nation is quite diverse.

◆Module 4　Scenario Link◆

Open.

▬▬▬▬▬ Tapescripts ▬▬▬▬▬

◆Module 1　Learn to Talk◆

Describing Places and Objects

3. *Listen to a conversation carefully and decide whether the following statements are true (T) or false (F).*

Tom:　Hi, Senina.

Senina:　Hi, Tom.

Tom:　Did you go to the party last night?

Senina:　Sure. How about you?

Tom:　I met some of our classmates at the gathering. But I didn't meet you.

Senina:　What a pity! But I met some our classmates too.

Tom:　Linda told me she will have a painting exhibition in Mogan Museum on March 18th. Do you want to go see it?

Senina:　Why not? I am interested in art. But I can't find the museum.

Tom:　Oh, it's very easy to find it. Go along this street to the second cross, then turn left and go straight to the first bus stop.

Senina: Wait, wait. What's the name of the bus stop?

Tom: Mogan.

Senina: Mogan? Oh. Absolutely, I can get there easily.

Tom: Hope to see you there at the art exhibition. We can see a lot of fantastic paintings by Linda.

Senina: Sure. See you next week.

Tom: See you.

Stories of Painters

Leonardo da Vinci was born on April 15th, 1452. He was a great inventor, scientist, engineer, writer, musician and one of the greatest painters of all time. He was born at Vinci, Florence. His father was Piero da Vinci and his mother was a peasant girl. Da Vinci worked in places like Venice and Rome, but he spent his final years in France at a place offered by the King Francois I. Leonardo da Vinci has been described as a great genius and we know him as the "Renaissance man". He is especially renowned for two of his works, *The Mona Lisa* and *The Last Supper*.

The Mona Lisa is an amazing sixteenth century portrait painting. It is the most famous painting in the world and few other works of art have been subject to as much study. Now, the painting is owned by the French government and kept at the Louvre Museum in Paris, France.

The Last Supper shows a scene of the last supper of Jesus Christ during his final days, when Jesus announced that one of his twelve followers would betray him. This painting can be found at the back of the dining hall at Santa Maria delle Grazie in Milan, Italy.

Raphael, called "the prince of painters", was born in Urbino, an artistic centre, on April 6th, 1483, and received his early training in art from his father, a poet and painter. His father recognised his son's enormous talent very early on and arranged his apprenticeship with Perugino. His father died when Raphael was only 11, but in 1500, at the age of only 17, Raphael was already considered a master. Raphael's early work reflects the style, clarity, and harmony that he learned from Perugino, and their paintings are so similar that even art experts have found it difficult to tell who painted what.

In 1504, Raphael moved to Florence where he studied from Da Vinci and Michelangelo. During these years, he drew numerous Madonnas. The sweet charm and grace of Raphael's Madonnas have been loved by the world ever since he painted them, and they are the works for which he is best remembered. Raphael died in Rome on his 37th birthday, April 6th, 1520.

Text Translations

◆ Passage A ◆

最多产的画家——帕巴洛·毕加索

西班牙画家帕巴洛·毕加索（1881 年 10 月 25 日—1973 年 4 月 8 日）是 20 世纪公认的艺术大师之一，也因和乔治·勃拉克一起成立了立体主义画派而蜚声海内外。

毕加索因和他人共同创立了立体主义画派而非常出名。然而，在他漫长的一生中，他也创作了广泛和变化多样的作品。其中最著名的是蓝色时期的作品，描绘了杂技演员、乞丐和艺术家的各种姿态。

毕加索也是《吉尼斯世界纪录大全》承认的最多产的画家。他创作了大约 13 500 幅绘画和设计，1 000 000 版画和雕刻，34 000 幅书籍插图，以及 300 个雕塑品，陶瓷和素描。在 1973 年，他的作品总价估计为 7 亿 5 千万美元。

毕加索最著名的作品是描述德国轰炸西班牙小镇格尔尼卡的一幅油画：《格尔尼卡》。这幅大型油画向众人展现了战争的非人道和绝望。毕加索最著名的爱人，本身也是一位杰出艺术家的多洛·玛尔用一系列照片记录了油画的创作过程。很多年来，《格尔尼卡》一直悬挂在纽约现代艺术馆。毕加索承诺，只有西班牙重建民主后，这幅画才能送回西班牙。1981 年，这幅画终于回归西班牙，并在马德里的莱蒂罗公园大宅中展出。1992 年，当马德里的瑞内索菲亚美术馆开馆时，这幅画成为该馆亮点之一。

◆ Passage B ◆

梵·高

1953 年 3 月 30 日，在荷兰南部的北布莱班特省的一个叫格如特—尊德特的小村子里，温森特·梵·高出生了。他的父亲瑟多瑞·梵·高是荷兰改革教会的牧师。温森特·梵·高和他祖父同名。在梵高家族，温森特是一个很普通的名字。他的祖父温森特于 1811 年在雷登大学获得神学学位。祖父有 6 个儿子，其中 3 个成为艺术商。所以艺术和宗教是梵高家族喜爱的两个职业。

梵·高刚成年后就为一家艺术交易公司工作，奔走于海牙、伦敦和巴黎之间，之后他又在英格兰教书。从 1879 年开始，他在比利时的矿区作传教士。这期间，他开始给当地人画素描。1886 年 3 月，他迁到巴黎并结交了法国的印象派画家。后来，他又搬到法国南部并被它强烈的阳光所吸引。他的作品在色彩上日趋明亮，并形成了独特而受到高度认可的风格。1888 年，当他待在阿尔镇时，这种风格完全成熟。

梵·高的作品色彩生动，情感丰沛，对 20 世纪的艺术产生了深远影响。但是他深受焦虑和日益频繁发作的精神疾病困扰，因此，当他 37 岁时，他开枪自杀，悄然离世。活着时，默默无闻，死后却日渐名气大涨。今天，他已被广泛认为是历史上最伟大的画家之一，并对现代艺术的形成作了重要贡献。

Unit 3　Actors and Actresses

I. Background Information

　　The ancient Greek word for an actor—hypocrites, means literally "one who interprets". In this sense, an actor is one who interprets a dramatic character or personality in film, television, theatre, or radio.

　　The first recorded case of an actor performing took place in 534 BC when the Greek performer Thespis stepped on the stage at the Theatre Dionysus and became the first known person to speak words as a character in a play or story. Before Thespis' act, stories were only known to be told in song and dance and in third person's narrative. In honor of Thespis, actors are commonly called Thespians.

　　In the past, only men could become actors in some societies. In the ancient Greece and Rome and the medieval world, it was considered disgraceful for a woman to go on the stage. In the time of William Shakespeare, women's roles were generally played by men or boys. This tradition continued right up until the 17th century, when it was broken in Venice.

　　When an eighteen-year Puritan prohibition of drama was lifted after the English Restoration of 1660, women began to appear on stage in England. This prohibition ended during the reign of Charles II in part due to the fact that he enjoyed watching actresses on stage. Margaret Hughes is credited as the first professional actress on the English stage. The first occurrence of the term "actress" was in 1700 according to the Oxford English Dictionary.

　　Actors were traditionally not people of high status, and in the Early Middle Ages travelling acting troupes were often viewed with distrust. In many parts of Europe, actors could not even receive a Christian burial, and traditional beliefs of the region and time period held that this left any actor forever condemned. However, this negative perception was largely reversed in the 19th and 20th centuries as acting has become an honored and popular profession and art.

　　Actors can be classified by the roles they play in performance.

- A lead (actor)—a star plays the principal role in a film or play;
- A support—a supporting actor performs roles in a play or film that range from bit parts to secondary leads.
- A bit part is a supporting actor with at least one line of dialogue. Unlike extras, actors in bit parts are typically listed in the credits. (A supporting role with no dialogue is called a walk-on).
- An extra (actor) is a performer who appears in nonspeaking, nonsinging or nondancing capacity, usually in the background (for example, in an audience or busy street scene).
- A character actor is one who predominantly plays a particular type of role. Character actor roles

can range from bit parts to secondary leads.

- A body double is a general term for someone who substitutes for the credited actor.
- A stuntman—a stunt double is someone who performs dangerous or sophisticated sequences in a play.

II. Notes

1. Notes to Lead-in

(1) Will Smith

威尔·史密斯(1968.9.25—)。美国演员、嘻哈歌手。他是少数在美国三大主要娱乐媒体——电影、电视和音乐方面同时获得成功的艺人。他曾以《拳王阿里》(*Ali*)和《当幸福来敲门》(*The Pursuit of Happiness*)分获 2002 年和 2007 年奥斯卡奖和金球奖提名。其代表作还有《独立日》(*Independence Day*)、《黑衣人》(*Men in Black*)、《全民公敌》(*Enemy of the State*)、《全民情敌》(*Hitch*)和《我,机器人》(*I, Robot*)、《新泽西女孩》(*Jersey Girl*)。同时,他在流行和嘻哈音乐领域也颇具知名度,最知名的曲目包括"*Men in Black*"、"*Gettin' Jiggy With It*"以及"*Just the Two of Us*"。

(2) Morgan Freeman

摩根·弗里曼(1937.6.1—)。美国演员、导演。出演过多部好莱坞电影。他成名于 20 世纪 80 年代后期,1987 年凭借在《浪迹街头》(*Street Smart*)中精湛演技获得当年奥斯卡最佳男配角和金球奖的两项提名。1989 年又以《为戴西小姐开车》(*Driving Miss Daisy*)赢得金球奖和全美影评奖。2005 年凭借《百万美元宝贝》(Million Dollar Baby)获得第 77 届奥斯卡最佳男配角奖。其代表作还有《光荣战役》(*Glory*)、《不可饶恕》(*Unforgiven*)、《肖申克的救赎》(*The Shawshank Redemption*)、《七宗罪》(*Seven*)、《冒牌天神》(*Bruce Almighty*)、《遗愿清单》(*The Bucket List*)、《赤焰战场》(*Red*)等。

(3) Halle Berry

哈里·贝瑞(1966.8.14—)。美国演员。20 世纪 80 年代开始演艺生涯,曾出演《色欲森林》(*Jungle Fever*)、《X 战警》(*X-Men*)、《择日而亡》(*Die Another Day*)、《猫女》(*Catwoman*)等片。她凭借在《死囚之舞》(*Monster's Ball*)中的出色表演赢得了第 74 届奥斯卡最佳女主角奖,成为史上第一位获此殊荣的黑人女演员。

(4) Eddie Murphy

埃迪·墨菲(1961.4.3—)。美国喜剧演员、歌手、配音员。他参演过许多著名的喜剧电影,包括《比佛利山超级警探》(*Beverly Hills Cop*),并因此片获得金球奖最佳喜剧男演员,以及《来到美国》(*Coming to America*)、《怪教授》(*Nutty Professor*)、《怪医杜立德》(*Doctor Dolittle*)、《人生》(*Life*)、《超级奶爸》(*Daddy Day Care*)、《糯米正传》(*Norbit*)。他也是著名的配音员,曾经为电影《怪物史莱克》(*Shrek*)系列里的驴子和迪士尼电影《花木兰》(*Mulan*)中的"木须"配音。

2. Notes to Module 1

(1) Danzel Washington

丹泽尔·华盛顿(1954.12.18—)。好莱坞最具票房号召力的演员之一,也是目前好莱坞身价最高的黑人影星。1990 年他凭借电影《光荣》(*Glory*)获得第 62 届奥斯卡最佳男配角奖,2000 年凭借电影《飓风》(*The Hurricane*)获得第 57 届金球奖最佳男主角奖(剧情类),2002 年凭借电影《训练日》(*Training Day*)获第 74 届奥斯卡最佳男主角奖,是继西德尼·波蒂埃(*Sidney Poitier*)后第二位黑人影帝。其代表作还有《生死豪情》(*Courage Under Fire*)、《纽约大爆炸》(*The Siege*)、《人骨拼图》(*The Bone Collector*)、《美国黑帮》(*American Gangster*)、《怒火救援》(*Man on Fire*)、《激辩风云》(*The Great Debaters*)、《艾利之书》(*The Book of Eli*)等。

(2) Hollywood

好莱坞,港译"荷里活"。位于美国加利福尼亚州洛杉矶市西北郊,是全球最著名的影视娱乐城市和旅游热门地点。现"好莱坞"一词往往直接用来指美国的电影工业。

(3) Academy Award

(美国)电影艺术与科学学院奖,即 Oscar,奥斯卡奖。1927 年 5 月,美国电影界知名人士在好莱坞发起组织一个"非营利组织",定名为 Academy of Motion Picture Arts and Science(电影艺术与科学学院),旨在促进电影艺术和技术的进步。学院决定对优秀电影工作者的显著成就给予表彰,因而成立了 Academy Award(电影艺术与科学学院奖)。1931 年后"学院奖"逐渐被其通俗叫法"奥斯卡金像奖"所代替。当前所设奖项可分成就奖和特别奖两大类。成就奖主要包括最佳影片奖、最佳剧本奖、最佳导演奖、最佳表演(男女主、配角)奖、最佳摄影奖、最佳美工奖、最佳音乐奖、最佳剪辑奖、最佳服装设计奖、最佳化妆奖、最佳短片奖、最佳纪录片奖、最佳动画片奖、最佳外语片奖等。特别奖则有荣誉奖、欧文撒尔伯格纪念奖、琼赫肖尔特人道主义奖、科技成果奖和特别成就奖。在上述众多奖项中,最具影响的是最佳影片奖和最佳男女主角奖。

3. Notes to Module 2

(1) Al Pacino

艾尔·帕西诺(1940.4.25—　)。美国著名电影演员。他在《教父》(*The Godfather*)系列中扮演的迈克·柯里昂是电影史上一个令人难忘的经典人物。1993 年,凭借在电影《闻香识女人》(*Scent of a Woman*)中的精湛演技,他获得了第 65 届奥斯卡最佳男演员奖和第 50 届金球奖最佳男主角奖(剧情类)。他 2007 年获得美国电影协会颁布的终身成就奖,这是演员生涯中最高的荣誉。

(2) Juliette Binoche

朱丽叶·比诺什(1964.3.9—　)。法国著名女演员。1986 年,她在《别了,布莱欧》(*Farewell blaireau*)中崭露头角,继而在 1988 年以影片《布拉格之恋》(*The Unbearable Lightness of Being*)一举成名。她所主演的影片几乎部部都是精品,代表作包括《新桥恋人》(*The Lovers On The Bridge*)、《蓝色情挑》(*Blue*)、《英国病人》(*The English Patient*)、《屋顶上的轻骑兵》(*The Horseman On The Roof*)、《浓情朱古力》(*Chocolate*)等。她赢得了无数国际大奖,除奥斯卡奖以外,她也是史上第一位获得欧洲恺撒电影节、戛纳电影节、威尼斯电影节三冠王的女演员。

(3) Krzysztof Kieslowski

克日什托夫·基耶斯洛夫斯基(1941.4.27—1996.3.13)。法籍波兰电影大师。他的影片被认为"既有伯格曼影片的诗情,又有希区柯克的叙事技巧"。他更被尊为"当代欧洲最具独创性、最有才华和最无所顾忌"的电影大师。代表作有《永无休止》(*No End*)、《十诫》(*The Decalogue*)、《蓝色情挑》(*Blue*)、《白色情迷》(*White*)、《红色情深》(*Red*)等。

（4）Steven Spielberg

史蒂芬·斯皮尔伯格（1946.12.18—　）。美国著名电影导演、编剧和电影制作人。他被誉为电影奇才，拍摄的电影题材广泛，包括犹太人大屠杀、奴隶制度、战争与恐怖主义等。他曾于 1993 年和 1998 年分别以《辛德勒的名单》（*Schindler's List*）和《拯救大兵瑞恩》（*Saving Private Ryan*）两度荣获奥斯卡最佳导演奖。其代表作还有《外星人》（*E. T*）、《大白鲨》（*Jaws*）、《紫色》（*The Color Purple*）、《太阳帝国》（*Empire of the Sun*）、《少数派报告》（*Minority Report*）、《猫鼠游戏》（*Catch Me If You Can*）、《幸福终点站》（*The Terminal*）等。在 2009 年，他被授予第 66 届美国电影电视金球奖终身成就奖。

（5）Cesar Award

法国（电影）恺撒奖。法国电影的最高荣誉，有"法国奥斯卡"之称。第一届于 1976 年 4 月 3 日由法国电影艺术与技术学会和法国电视二台合作举办。奖项由组织评选投票产生，每年一届。最初，恺撒奖设有"最佳法国片奖"、"最佳导演奖"、"最佳男女主角奖"、"最佳男女配角奖"、"最佳编剧奖"、"最佳原创音乐奖"、"最佳摄影奖"、"最佳布景奖"、"最佳音效奖"、"最佳剪辑奖"、"最佳记录片奖"以及"最佳外语片奖"等 13 个单项奖。随后，逐步增设"最佳服装奖"和"最佳短片奖"。1982 年开始增设"最佳处女作奖"。1983 年为纪念 *Romy Schneider* 和 *Patrick Deweare* 又分别增设"最佳男女新人奖"，但与此同时取消了"最佳海报"和"最佳制片人"两个奖项，因此如今的恺撒奖共设 20 个奖项。恺撒奖的颁奖典礼于每年的 2 月底或 3 月初在法国巴黎举行。

（6）Venice Film Festival

威尼斯电影节。威尼斯电影节号称"国际电影节之父"。1932 年 8 月 6 日在意大利名城威尼斯创办，主要目的在于提高电影艺术水平。1934 年举办第 2 届后每年 8 月底至 9 月初举行一次，为期两周。1932—1942 年，奖项分为最佳故事片、纪录片、短片、意大利影片、外国影片，以及最佳导演、编剧、男女演员、摄影、音乐等奖。此外，还有特别奖、综合奖、"双年节杯"等。1949 年增设"圣马克金狮奖"、"圣马克银狮奖"、"圣马克铜狮奖"等。威尼斯电影节与德国的柏林电影节、法国的戛纳电影节、加拿大的多伦多国际电影节以及捷克的卡罗维发利电影节是国际电影联合会认可的国际五大电影节；也是世界四大艺术电影节之一（德国柏林电影节、意大利威尼斯电影节、法国戛纳国际电影节、俄罗斯莫斯科电影节）。

（7）Cannes Festival

戛纳电影节。戛纳电影节是世界最大、最重要的电影节之一。1939 年，法国为了对抗当时受意大利法西斯政权控制的威尼斯国际电影节，决定创办法国自己的国际电影节。第二次世界大战爆发使筹备工作停顿下来。大战结束后，于 1946 年 9 月 20 日在法国南部旅游胜地戛纳举办了首届电影节。自创办以来，除 1948 年、1950 年停办和 1968 年中途断外，每年举行一次，为期两周左右。原来每年 9 月举行，1951 年起，为了在时间上争取早于威尼斯国际电影节而改在 5 月举行。1956 年最高奖为"金鸭奖"，1957 年起改为"金棕榈奖"，分别授予最佳故事片、纪录片、科教片、美术片等。此外，历年来还先后颁发过爱情心理电影、冒险侦探电影、音乐电影、传记片、娱乐片、处女作、导演、男女演员、编剧、摄影、剪辑等奖。

4. Notes to Module 3

Table manners are the rules of etiquette while eating, which may also include the proper use of utensils. Whether you are eating at a fancy restaurant, in the cafeteria or at home with friends and families, good table manners make for a more pleasant meal.

While you may not want to worry about confusing your salad fork with your desert fork when dining with friends, some basic table manners should never be forgotten. Here are some easy-to-follow rules.

Dinnerware rules:

- Eat to your left, drink to your right. Any food dish to the left is yours, and any glass to the right is yours;
- Start with the knife, fork, or spoon that is farthest from your plate, work your way in, using one utensil for each course;
- Keep both knife and fork in your hands with point curved downward throughout the entire eating process;
- Follow one of the two methods when using fork and knife. American style: knife in right hand and fork in left hand holding food. After a few bite-sized pieces of food are cut, put knife on edge of plate with blades facing in. Eat food by switching fork to right hand (unless you are left-handed). Continental/European style: knife in right hand, fork in left hand. Eat food with fork still in left hand;
- Put both knife and fork down if you take a drink;
- Leave plates and glasses (both used and not used) where they are when you are finished rather than stack them for the waiter;
- To signal that your are done with the course, rest your fork, tines up, and knife blade in, with the handles resting at five o'clock and tips pointing to ten o'clock on your plate.

More Do's:

- Turn off your cell phone or switch it to silent or vibrate mode before sitting down to eat. If you must make or take a call, excuse yourself from the table and step outside of the restaurant;
- Sit up straight in your chair;
- Wait until everyone is seated before starting to eat;
- Place your napkin on your lap;
- Keep elbows off the table;
- Talk about cheerful, pleasant things at the table;
- Cut only enough food for the next mouthful;
- Chew with your mouth closed;
- Scoop food away from you;
- Ask someone to pass the food or seasoning rather than reach across the table;
- Cover your mouth with your napkin if you cough, sneeze or blow your nose;
- Try to pace your eating so that you don't finish before others are halfway through;
- Say "Excuse me" or "I'm sorry" before leaving the table halfway;
- Say "No, thank you" if you don't want a certain dish or are full.

More Don't s:

- Don't talk with food in your mouth;
- Don't blow on your food to cool it off;
- Don't wave your tableware in the air or point with it;
- Don't make eating noises such as slurping or burping;
- Don't eat with or lick your fingers;
- Don't overload your fork or plate;
- Don't sip your soup but swallow it;
- Don't touch items that have dropped on the floor;
- Don't play with your food or utensils;
- Don't use a toothpick or apply make‑up at the table.

III. Language Points

▬▬▬ Passage A ▬▬▬

◆ Important Words ◆

major[ˈmeɪdʒə(r)] *a.* of great importance or status or rank 主要的；较大的；*n.* a university student who is studying a particular field as the principal subject 专业；*v.* to have sth as one's principal field of study 专修、专攻

e. g.   1. Age is a major factor that affects chances of employment.

2. He has great interest in history and so chose history as his major at college.

3. What do you think he is majoring in.

breakthrough[ˈbreɪkθruː] *n.* a discovery or achievement that comes after a lot of hard work 突破性发展；成就

e. g.   1. Scientists predict a major breakthrough within six months.

2. It was the breakthrough that he needed if he wanted to win the game.

release[rɪˈliːs] *vt.* to make a film, video, or CD available for people to see or buy 发行；上映；to let someone leave a place where they have been kept 释放；to stop holding something 放开、松开；to get rid of a negative feeling 缓解、松弛

e. g.   1. They have just released their second album.

2. The pirates promised to release two more hostages next week.

3. She slowly released her grip on my hand.

4. Do you know how to release pressure efficiently?

virtually[ˈvɜːtʃuəli] almost 几乎、差不多；in fact, actually 实际上、事实上

e. g.　1. Virtually all the students live in university halls of residence.

2. It's virtually impossible to persuade him to eat any vegetable.

challenge[ˈtʃælɪndʒ]*vt.* to invite someone to compete or fight 挑战; to test one's skills or ability 尝试; to question whether sth is true, accurate or legal 质疑; *n.* sth that needs a lot of skill, energy and determination to deal with 挑战

e. g.　1. He will challenge a totally new role in the next play.

2. The girls challenged boys to a cricket match.

3. They are not likely to challenge us on any of the details.

4. I was bored with my job and felt I needed new challenges.

review[rɪˈvjuː]*n.* an article someone gives their opinion of a play or book 评论; the process of studying or examining a situation, policy or idea again 回顾、重新考虑; a practice intended to polish knowledge or refresh memory 复习

e. g.　1. The film also won great reviews in America.

2. Several aspects of this program are now under review.

3. We will have a review of chapters three and four.

recover[rɪˈkʌvə]*vt.* to get back the ability to do or feel sth 恢复、重新获得; to become fit or healthy again after an illness or injury 康复、痊愈

e. g.　1. He never recovered the use of his arm after the crash.

2. I haven't fully recovered from that flu I had.

popular[ˈpɒpjələ(r)]*a.* (of somebody or sth) being liked by most people 流行的; 受欢迎的; (of ideas or beliefs) being shared or held by many people 普遍的

e. g.　1. He is very popular with critics and audience.

2. It's a popular misconception that all women love shopping.

previous[ˈpriːviəs]*a.* happening or existing before the one somebody is having or talking about 先前的,以前的

e. g.　1. This problem was discussed in the previous chapter.

2. Previous to his present employment he was a bus driver.

incredible[ɪnˈkredəbl]*a.* impossible or very difficult to believe 不可思议的;难以置信的

e. g.　1. It seemed incredible that she had been there a week already.

2. Michael told us an incredible story about his grandmother catching a thief.

produce[prə'djuːs]*vt.* to bring out a film, play or book 创作、演出；to create or manufacture 生产、制造；to give birth or yield 生育、产出

e.g.　1. The fresh Academy Award winner will produce two new films next year.

　　　2. The factory has been producing toys for two centuries.

　　　3. The tree doesn't produce fruits.

◆ Explanation of Difficult Sentences ◆

(1) Pcino went from being a nobody to international star virtually overnight.

- 几乎一夜之间帕西诺就从一个无名小卒变成了世界巨星。
- nobody 在此作名词，意为"小人物、无名小卒"，其反义词是"somebody 大人物，名人"。

(2) Although he could have settled for easy acting roles, Pacino went on to challenge himself with some of Hollywood's most difficult roles, …, which showed his versatility as an actor.

- 帕西诺原本可以稳稳当当地演些容易的角色，但他却继续挑战自己尝试出演好莱坞一些高难度的角色，……这些角色显示了他宽阔的戏路。
- could have done 表示"原本可以做却没做"。定语从句的引导词 which 此处代指 some of Hollywood's most difficult roles.

(3) In 1989, he starred in *Sea of Love*, which was great success.

- 1989 年他主演了《午夜惊情》，该片获得了巨大成功。
- star 在此作动词，意为"担当主演"。

(4) With his incredible emotion and powerful performances, Pacino has produced an unbeatable number of classic roles and become a legend in American film history.

- 帕西诺有着惊人的激情和富有张力的表演，他塑造了无数经典角色，成为美国电影史上的传奇人物。
- with 引导的介词结构在此表示原因。

Passage B

◆ Important Words ◆

leading['liːdɪŋ]*a.* main 主要的；most important or most successful 最重要的、最成功的

e.g.　1. This is a leading brand of toothpaste in the local market.

　　　2. The leading cause of this accident was the carelessness of the driver.

gain[geɪn]*vt.* to get or achieve sth, usually with a lot of effort 获得、赢得

e.g.　1. She hopes to gain experience by working abroad for a year.

　　　2. His first novel gained unexpected success and now he is engaged in the second.

alike[ə'laɪk]*ad.* equally 同样地、两者都; *a.* living and not dead 活着的

e. g.　1. It's a show that attracts the young and the old alike.

　　　2. He was lucky to be alive after the earthquake.

extend[ɪk'stend]*vt.* to offer sth formally 给予;提供; to continue for a distance or a period of time 延伸、延长

e. g.　1. We extend our apologies for the inconvenience caused.

　　　2. The industrial zone extends along the river.

　　　3. The festival will extend over a period of weeks.

offer['ɒfə]*n.* proposal 提议、意向; *vt.* to give sth to someone 给与、提供

e. g.　1. After thinking about it, I decided to accept your offer.

　　　2. They haven't offered me the job.

rising['raɪzɪŋ]*a.* becoming higher or greater in degree, value or status 上升的、成长中的

e. g.　1. They have great interest in the rising Asian market.

　　　2. The rising political star attracted the worldwide attention.

embrace[ɪm'breɪs]*vt.* to accept sth completely and happily (欣然)接受; to hug 拥抱

e. g.　1. Now most countries have embraced the concept of high-speed railways.

　　　2. He embraced me warmly to show how happy he was to see me again.

award[ə'wɔːd]*vt.* to give someone a prize 授予、奖给; *n.* prize 奖品

e. g.　1. Students who complete the course successfully will be awarded a diploma.

　　　2. Unexpectedly she won the first award in the speech contest.

title['taɪtl]*vt.* to name or entitle 称为;赋予头衔; *n.* the name of a book, poem, film or other work of art 标题、题目; a word or name that is used before one's name to show their profession or social status 头衔

e. g.　1. Her first novel, titled *More Innocent Times*, was published in 1997.

　　　2. What's the title of this play?

　　　3. His new title is vice president.

◆Explanation of Difficult Sentences◆

(1) The film premiered at the 1993 Venice Film Festival, where she was landed a best actress prize.

- 这部电影在 1993 年威尼斯电影节上首映,她因此片荣获该届电影节最佳女演员奖。
- where 引导的定语从句修饰先行词 Venice Film Festival。

(2) Soon came the production *The English Patient*.

- 接踵而至的就是电影《英国病人》。
- 该句采用了倒装结构,谓语 came 被提到了主语 the production *The English Patient* 之前。

(3) Binoche's most notable performances also include… and *Certified Copy*, for which she received the Best Actress award at the 2010 Cannes Film Festival, making her the first actress in history to win the European "triple crown".

- 比诺什最出名的作品还包括……和《爱情对白》。《爱情对白》一片为她赢得了 2010 年戛纳电影节最佳女主角殊荣,她成为史上第一位获得欧洲三大电影节桂冠的女演员。
- for which 是"介词 + which"引导的定语从句修饰 *Certified Copy*。

IV. Keys, Tapescripts and Text Translations

Keys

◆Lead-in◆

1. (From left to right): Will Smith, Morgan Freeman, Halle Berry, Eddie Murphy
2. Denzel Washington.

◆Module 1   Learn to Talk◆

Where Can I Get It

1. *Lisa meets her colleague Susan at the pantry room(茶水间)and asks her where she can buy art supplies. Listen to it and think about the following questions.*
   (1) Yes, she is very polite.
   (2) Because she uses the expression "I was wondering if you could help".

2. *Listen to the dialogue again and fill in the missing words in the blanks.*

(1) Hi	(2) I was wondering if you could help me	(3) Let me see
(4) Well	(5) I hope you don't mind my askig	(6) I see

3. Open.

4. *Work with your partner and decide whether the following questions would be appropriate to ask if you're talking with a native English speaker you've just met. Mark "Y" for "Yes" and "N" for "No".*

(1)N   (2)Y   (3)N   (4)Y   (5)Y   (6)N   (7)Y   (8)N   (9)N

(10)Y   (11)Y   (12)Y   (13)Y   (14)N   (15)N   (16)N   (17)Y   (18)N

5. Open.   6. Open.

Stories of Denzel Washington

While You Listen

1. *Listen and decide whether the following statements about Denzel Washington are true (T) or false (F).*

(1)F   (2)F   (3)T   (4)F   (5)F

2. *Listen again and fill in the following table about Denzel Washington's achievements and the reasons for his success.*

Achievements	(1) He won great awards for his work, including __2__ Academy Awards, __3__ nominations and at least fifty other awards.
	(2) In 2007 his average wage was $20 million per picture.
Reasons	(1) He possesses a very important quality: integrity.
	(2) He is not restricted to one type of role only, but is a versatile actor.
	(3) He has a very happy family with __4__ children.

After You Listen

Open.

◆Module 2   Learn to Read◆

Warm-up

Open.

Passage A   A Legend in American Film Industry–Al Pacino

Reading Comprehension

1. *Global understanding*

(1) Al Pacino is one of the greatest actors in American film industry.

(2) Factual

2. *Detailed understanding*

(1)A   (2)C   (3)B   (4)A   (5)D

Language Practice

1. *Make sure you know the words in the table below. Choose the proper word to complete each of the following sentences. Change the form where necessary.*

(1) decade   (2) popular   (3) starring   (4) breakthrough   (5) had supported

(6) previous   (7) virtually   (8) incredible   (9) performance   (10) recover

2. *Each of the verbs and nouns in the following lists occurs in the passage. Match the verbs and nouns to make proper collocations.*

to make a debut   to play a role   to release a film

to gain attention   to earn an award

3. *Translate the following pairs of sentences, paying special attention to the coloured parts.*

(1) a. 年龄是影响就业机会的一个主要因素。

b. 对于大多数计划出国留学的中国学生而言,专业的选择是其重点关注的事情。

(2) a. 这支乐队刚发行了他们的第二张专辑。

b. 这些鸟会被放归野外,因为它们已完全康复。

(3) a. 我对这份工作感到厌倦,觉得需要新的挑战。

b. 我认为他错了,所以对他提出质疑。

(4) a. 这所大学出版了一本戏剧评论。

b. 政府将对其所有环保政策进行检讨。

(5) a. 他是一个天才的小说家,已经出版了好几本著名的作品。

b. 这条新的生产线每年将出产十万辆轿车。

Passage B   French Beauty–Juliette Binoche

Reading Comprehension

1. *Global understanding*

(1) Juliette Binoche's successful career and her adventurous characteristic.

(2) Admiring.

2. *Detailed understanding*

(1) T   (2) F   (3) T   (4) F   (5) F   (6) F   (7) F   (8) F   (9) T   (10) T

Language Practice

1. *Match the word in Column A with the appropriate meanings in Column B.*

(1) d   (2) e   (3) a   (4) c   (5) b

2. *Find the adjective forms for the following words in the passage.*

(1) fame—famous   (2) lead—leading

(3) rise—rising   (4) support—supporting

(5) note—notable   (6) adventure—adventurous

(7) know—unknown   (8) admire—admirable

3. *Complete the following sentences by translating into English the Chinese given in brackets.*

(1) later in this year   (2) including two children   (3) in which men solve problems

(4) speaking and laughing   (5) I have not seen her

◆Module 3　Culture Link◆

Quiz

1. *Read the following statements about table manners carefully and decide whether or not they are appropriate. Mark "Y" for "Yes" and "N" for "No".*

（1）Y　　（2）N　　（3）Y　　（4）N　　（5）Y　　（6）N　　（7）Y　　（8）N　　（9）N

（10）N　（11）N　（12）N　（13）Y　（14）N　（15）N

■ Tapescripts ■

◆Module 1　Learn to Talk◆

Where Can I Get It

Lisa: Hi! Susan!

Susan: Oh hi, Lisa!

Lisa: I was wondering if you could help me, but I'd like to know whether there's a good place nearby to by art supplies?

Susan: I'm not really sure. Let me see. Oh yeah, there's that new place, Mixed Media. You know it's on the Main Street?

Lisa: Mm, I don't know that store. Exactly where on Main Street?

Susan: Well, you know where the vegetarian restaurant is. It's right up the block.

Lisa: Oh yes. I know where you mean now.

Susan: Hey, I hope you don't mind my asking, but are you taking up painting?

Lisa: No! I can't paint. I'm just asking for my sister's son. He's really into it.

Susan: Ah, I see. Are you still doing your photography?

Lisa: Yeah, that's the thing I really enjoy.

Susan: Mm, you're really good at it.

Story of Denzel Washington

DENZEL WASHINGTON, the star of *American Gangster* and *The Great Debaters*, topped the list for the second year as America's favourite movie star in a new survey.

There have been very few actors over the past two decades who can claim to be as influential and respected as Washington. In American movie world, most black actors are generally restricted to one type of role-either action movie stars or comedy figures, but Denzel Washington stands alongside Morgan Freeman and Will Smith as one of the most versatile actors in Hollywood.

Sure, he has won great awards for his work (two Academy Awards, three nominations and at least fifty other awards), makes millions of dollars (in 2007, his average wage was $20 million per picture), and is attractive to the opposite sex, but there is a quality he possesses that is more important than any of these: integrity.

Washington is well known for not taking part in any of the usual entertainments that Hollywood stars are crazy about. He has been happily married to his wife since 1983 and has four children. Washington is an example of a popular figure whose public and private lives are kept distinctly separate.

Text Translations

◆ Passage A ◆

美国电影史上的传奇人物——阿尔·帕西诺

1969 年,阿尔·帕西诺首次出现在电影银幕上,在《我,娜塔丽》中演了个小角色。随后又在 1971 年主演了《毒海鸳鸯》。1972 年帕西诺出演了《教父》中迈克·卡利厄里一角,迎来了演艺事业上的突破。该片一经上映就获得了巨大成功,甚至引起了奥斯卡奖的关注。他因该片而获得奥斯卡最佳男配角提名。几乎一夜之间帕西诺就从一个无名小卒变成了世界巨星。

帕西诺原本可以稳稳当当地演些容易的角色,但他却继续尝试好莱坞电影中一些高难度的角色,如《冲突》中的警察、《热天午后》中的银行劫匪、《伸张正义》中的律师,这些角色展现了他宽阔的戏路。

《虎口巡航》(1980)和《欢喜冤家》(1982)票房惨败,恶评连连,帕西诺的演艺事业因此陷入低潮。但1983 年他凭借《疤面煞星》成功复出,铸造了一个经典的恶棍形象,其后多年还为人们津津乐道。

1989 年帕西诺担纲主演了《午夜惊情》,该片获得了巨大成功并开启了他演艺生涯的辉煌 10 年。在此期间,他主演了《教父Ⅲ》《至尊神探》《拜金一族》和《闻香识女人》。在他七获奥斯卡提名后,《闻香识女人》最终让他问鼎奥斯卡影帝的宝座。

帕西诺有着惊人的激情和富有张力的表演,他塑造了无数经典角色,成为美国电影史上的传奇人物。

◆ Passage B ◆

法国丽人——朱丽叶·比诺什

朱丽叶·比诺什,法国著名女演员,自 1985 年起出演过 40 多部电影。

1985 年在安德烈·泰西内执导的法国电影《情陷夜巴黎》中比诺什首次饰演女主角,次年就因该片第一次获得恺撒奖提名,享誉世界。

同年晚些时候,比诺什在《布拉格之恋》中出演特瑞莎。这是她第一个用英语诠释的角色,获得了全球影评界和观众的一致好评。

几年之后,两位知名导演——克日什托夫·基耶斯洛夫斯基和史蒂芬·斯皮尔伯格都向这位冉冉升起的新星发出了邀请。最终比诺什出演了基耶洛夫斯基的《三色之蓝色情挑》。该片在 1993 年威尼斯电影节上首映,她因此片荣获该届电影节最佳女演员奖。

接踵而至的就是《英国病人》。这部电影在全球取得了巨大成功,赢得了 9 项奥斯卡大奖,其中包括比诺什获得的最佳女配角奖。

比诺什最出名的作品还包括《浓情巧克力》《躲藏》《红气球》和《爱情对白》。《爱情对白》一片为她赢得了 2010 年戛纳电影节最佳女主角殊荣,她成为史上第一位获得欧洲三大电影节桂冠的女演员。

比诺什喜欢冒险。她说"我喜欢未知,这会激起我们内心的恐惧。拥抱恐惧是一种绝妙的感受"。表演、绘画、写作,现在又是舞蹈。45 岁时比诺什又展现出了令人敬佩的勇气。她和一个名为 in-i 的现代舞团开始了世界巡演。比诺什的确在实践着"我的生活我作主"。

Unit 4　Dancers

I. Background Information

Dance is an art form that generally refers to movement of the body used as a form of expression, social interaction or presented in a spiritual or performance setting. Every dance, no matter what style, has something in common. It not only involves flexibility and body movement, but also physics. Education in music, literature, history, and the arts can help you understand the mood and ideas of a dance.

Dancers express ideas, stories, rhythm, and sound with their bodies. Some dance in ballet; others perform modern dance. Dancers work in musical shows, in folk, ethnic, tap, and jazz dances. Opera, musical comedy, television, movies, music videos, and commercials often include dancing as well. Many dancers sing and act, as well as dance. Dancers often work as a group, but a few stars dance solo. Many dancers also teach or choreograph dances.

Choreographers (舞蹈编导) create new dances. They may also add changes to older dances. Some teach dancers to get the results they want. They may also rehearse dancers for a particular production.

Dancing is hard work. Rehearsals can be long and usually take place daily, even on weekends and holidays. Weekend travel is common when a show is on the road. Dancers must also work late hours and practice during the day. Because dancing is hard work, most dancers stop working by their late thirties. Sometimes they become dance teachers and coaches.

To become a dancer, one must be agile (活泼), flexible, have good body tone, and a supple (柔软) body. Training begins at age 5 to 8 in ballet, usually by private teachers and in ballet schools. Boys often start training later than girls. Students who are good by their early teens get more advanced training. Most dancers have their professional auditions (试演) by age 17 or 18. By then dancers usually focus on a specific style of dance. Dancers normally spend 8 hours a day in class and rehearsal, keeping their bodies in shape and preparing for performances.

Many exceptional dancers, past and present, have graced dance floors with their talents. They have forever changed the face of dance and continue to shape it today. Not only have they mastered their chosen art form, they have also paved pathways for future dancers, and entertained the rest of us. Though not complete, this unit highlights some of the best dancers of the past by showing the extent of their love of and devotion to their particular styles of dance.

II. Notes

1. Notes to Lead-in

Margot Fonteyn 玛戈特·芳婷,英国女芭蕾演员。1919 年 5 月 18 日生于萨里郡的赖盖特。在中国和美国度过童年,并开始学习芭蕾。1934 年返回英国,进入芭蕾舞学校学习。她在《胡桃夹子》中饰演小雪花,获得成功。后与阿什顿、麦克米伦合作,演出了《仙女之吻》《玫瑰幽灵》《睡美人》等,特别成功的是在 1961 年与纽里耶夫合作演出的《天鹅湖》、和麦克米伦重新创作的《罗密欧与朱丽叶》,以及和阿什顿的《玛格丽特和阿芒》。她的舞姿轻盈,能将音乐与舞蹈融为一体,举手投足都富于表情。她对芭蕾艺术态度认真,不断地追求和探索,直到息影舞台。芳婷在 1956 年获"女爵士"称号,是英国皇家舞蹈学院名誉院长。1979 年访问中国,将北京舞蹈学院演出的《卖火柴的小女孩》编入她与英国 BBC 电视台合拍的自传片中。

2. Notes to Module 1

(1) Carl Sandburg

卡尔·桑伯格(1878—1967),美国 20 世纪最伟大的诗人和作家之一,是美国作家当中继沃尔特·惠特曼之后唯一能被称为"人民的诗人"的诗人。在诗歌创作上,他师承了惠特曼的自由体诗歌的文体形式,沿用了长句的写作风格,以及罗列人、事和物的写作技巧,采用人民的语言创作以及诗歌里重复和平行结构的修辞手段,从而进一步使自由体诗歌更加为人民所接受,也在极大程度上体现了亲民性。

(2) the Great Depression

大萧条,指 1929 年至 1933 年之间全球性的经济大衰退。

(3) the Spanish Civil War

西班牙内战(1936 年 7 月 18 日—1939 年 4 月 1 日),是在西班牙第二共和国发生的一场内战,由共和国总统曼努埃尔·阿扎尼亚的共和政府军与人民阵线左翼联盟对抗以弗朗西斯科·佛朗哥为中心的西班牙国民军和长枪党等右翼集团。反法西斯的人民阵线和共和政府有苏联和墨西哥的援助,而佛朗哥的国民军则有纳粹德国、意大利王国和葡萄牙的支持。西班牙内战被认为是第二次世界大战发生的前奏。

(4) the Presidential Medal of Freedom

总统自由勋章,是由美国总统向在科学、文化、体育和社会活动等领域作出杰出贡献的平民颁发的一种勋章,是美国对普通人的最高奖励。总统自由勋章最早于 1945 年由杜鲁门总统创立,以表彰那些在二战中有杰出贡献的平民,1963 年肯尼迪总统重新推出了这个颁奖活动,修改为授予在和平时期有杰出贡献的平民。

3. Notes to Module 2

(1) Cixi

慈禧(叶赫那拉·杏贞)太后,1835 年 11 月 29 日(道光十五年十月十日)—1908 年 11 月 15 日(光绪三十四年十月二十二日),又称"西太后"、"那拉太后"、"老佛爷",死后清朝谥号为"孝钦慈禧端佑康颐昭豫庄诚寿恭钦献崇熙配天兴圣显皇后",为有史以来皇后生后哀荣之最。慈禧是清朝政府腐败、软弱、无能、残暴的代表。是 1861 年至 1908 年间清朝的实际统治者。

(2) *Sleeping Beauty*

《睡美人》,柴可夫斯基作曲,俄国最杰出的芭蕾舞大师马留斯·彼季帕编导的芭蕾舞剧。被赞誉为"古典芭蕾的巅峰之作"，世界三大经典芭蕾舞剧之一。

(3) *Swan Lake*

《天鹅湖》，柴可夫斯基的芭蕾舞剧，作于 1876 年。世界三大经典芭蕾舞剧之一。

(4) *Giselle*

浪漫主义芭蕾舞剧的代表作，得到了"芭蕾之冠"的赞美。这部舞剧第一次使芭蕾的女主角同时面临表演技能和舞蹈技巧两个方面的严峻挑战。舞剧是既富传奇性，又具世俗性的爱情悲剧，从中可以看到浪漫主义的两个侧面，光明与黑暗、生存与死亡。在第一幕中充满田园风光，第二幕又以超自然的想象展开各种舞蹈，特别是众幽灵的女子群舞更成为典范之作。一个半世纪以来，著名的芭蕾女演员都以演出《吉赛尔》做为最高的艺术追求。

(5) Alicia Markova

艾丽西亚·玛尔科娃女爵士（1910—2004），英国芭蕾舞女演员。她最得意的角色是《吉赛尔》中的主角。玛尔科娃原名莉莲·艾丽西亚·马克斯，14 岁进入谢尔盖·佳吉列夫的俄罗斯芭蕾舞团。1941—1948 年间在芭蕾舞剧院和其他美国舞团跳舞，此后加入伦敦的节日芭蕾舞团。玛尔科娃退出舞台生涯后，于 1963—1969 年担任大都会歌剧院芭蕾舞团总监，1970 年开始在辛辛那提大学音乐学院任教，1963 年受封大英帝国爵级司令勋章，著有自传体作品《吉赛尔与我》（1960 年）和《玛尔科娃回忆录》（1986 年）。

(6) Dame Commander of the British Empire

大英帝国爵级司令勋章，为大英帝国勋章（Order of the British Empire）中的第二个级别。大英帝国勋章是英国授勋及嘉奖制度中的一种骑士勋章，由英王乔治五世于 1917 年 6 月 4 日所创立。勋章分民事和军事两类，共设 5 种级别，分别为

- 爵级大十字勋章（Knight/Dame Grand Cross，男女皆简称"GBE"）
- 爵级司令勋章（Knight/Dame Commander，男性简称"KBE"，女性简称"DBE"）
- 司令勋章（Commander，简称"CBE"）
- 官佐勋章（Officer，简称"OBE"）
- 员佐勋章（Member，简称"MBE"）

在上面五等中，只有获最上两等的授勋英国或英联邦王国公民才算取得骑士爵位，可以在他们的英文名称前加上"Sir/Dame"头衔，或在他们的中文名称后加上"爵士/女爵士"头衔。如果有外国公民获最上两等的勋衔，他们只可当作名誉性质，并不能冠上任何头衔。

(7) Rudolf Nureyev

鲁道夫·纽瑞耶夫（1938—1993），前苏联著名芭蕾舞演员。在今天，他与 Vaslav Nijinsky（瓦斯拉夫·尼金斯基）、Mikhail Baryshnikov（米凯亚·巴里什尼可夫）并称为 20 世纪最伟大的三大芭蕾舞男演员。

4. Notes to Module 3

(1) Body language

Body language is a form of non-verbal communication, which consists of body posture, gestures, facial expressions, and eye movements. Humans send and interpret such signals almost entirely subconsciously.

John Borg attests that human communication consists of 93 percent body language and para-linguistic cues, while only 7% of communication consists of words themselves; however, Albert Mehrabian, the researcher whose 1960's work is the source of these statistics, has stated that this is a misunderstanding of the findings. Others assert that "Research has suggested that between 60 and 70 percent of all meaning is derived from non-verbal behavior."

Body language may provide clues as to the attitude or state of mind of a person. For example, it may indicate aggression, attentiveness, boredom, relaxed state, pleasure, amusement, and intoxication, among many other cues.

(2) President Clinton and Monica Lewinsky

The president Clinton was threatened with removal from office after a sexual relationship with a young woman became public.

It started when a former Arkansas state employee took legal action against President Clinton in 1994. She charged that he had asked her for sex while he was governor of Arkansas. A federal judge dismissed her case for lack of evidence. But her lawyers wanted to prove that Mr. Clinton had had sex with several female workers. They suspected these included a young woman, Monica Lewinsky, who had worked as a White House assistant.

Earlier, Miss Lewinsky and Mr. Clinton had separately answered questions from lawyers. Both of them denied having a sexual relationship. In January of 1998, Mr. Clinton also denied publicly that he had a sexual relationship with Miss Lewinsky.

Six months later, Mr. Clinton agreed to answer questions before a federal investigating jury. He told the grand jury about his relationship with Lewinsky. This meant he had lied during earlier official questioning. That night, the president admitted on national television that he had had a relationship with Monica Lewinsky that was wrong. He told the nation his actions were a personal failure. But he denied trying to get her to lie about the relationship.

Bill Clinton remained president of the United States. But the forty-second president had hoped to be remembered for his leadership and the progress made during his administration. Instead, many people said he will be remembered for the charges against him.

III. Language Points

■■■■■ Passage A ■■■■■

◆ Important Words ◆

ambassador [æmˈbæsədə] *n.* an important official who represents his or her government in a foreign country 大使

e. g.　1. The ambassador held a reception at the embassy.

　　　2. The college gave the ambassador an honorary degree.

achievement[ə'tʃiːvmənt]*n.* sth important that you succeed in doing by your own efforts 成就；成绩

e. g.   1. I can't say how delighted I am about your achievement in biology.

2. Scientific/Educational achievement.

profession[prə'feʃn]*n.* a job that needs a high level of education and training 职业；行业

e. g.   1. She intends to make teaching her profession.

2. He's a lawyer by profession.

confront[kən'frʌnt]*vt.* to deal with sth very difficult or unpleasant in a brave and determined way 对抗；面对

e. g.   1. People who confront their difficulties bravely are people who face their difficulties bravely and try to succeed despite them.

2. We must confront the future with optimism.

persuade[pə'sweɪd]*vt.* to make someone decide to do sth, especially by giving them reasons why they should do it, or asking them many times to do it 劝说，说服

e. g.   1. I'll persuade him to join our club.

2. Couldn't I persuade you to stay a couple of days more?

institute['ɪnstɪtjuːt]*n.* an organization that has a particular purpose such as scientific or educational work 机构；学院

e. g.   1. I like your institute but I do not want to enroll.

2. I live at Beijing Broadcasting Institute.

be appointed as 被任命为……

e. g.   1. John was appointed as the chairman of the Trade Union.

2. The politician was appointed as the Minister of Finance.

be satisfied with 对……满意

e. g.   1. He can't pick and choose what job he wants nowadays; he must be satisfied with what he's offered.

2. Such a most talented person as he shouldn't be satisfied with what he is.

be nominated as 被任命为……

e. g.   1. The board nominated him as the new director.

2. She had been nominated as the candidate for the presidency.

49

◆ Explanation of Difficult Sentences ◆

(1) In Paris, she learned from the famous American dancer Isadora Duncan, who was then performing and teaching in Paris.

- 在巴黎,她师从当时在巴黎演出和教学的美国著名舞蹈家伊莎多拉·邓肯。

- who was then performing and teaching in Paris 是 who 引导的非限制性定语从句。

(2) Her father didn't allow her daughter to be a dancer, which was regarded as a base profession at that time.

- 她的父亲不容许自己的女儿成为舞蹈演员。这在当时被看作是低贱的职业。

- 本句为 which 引导的非限制性定语从句。非限制性定语从句的作用是对所修饰的成分作进一步说明, 通常是引导词和先行词之间用逗号隔开,将从句拿掉后其他部分仍可成立。

(3) Later, she studied more in the Paris Music Institute and staged more public performances.

- 后来裕容龄在巴黎音乐学院进一步深造并参加了更多的舞台表演。

- stage 的常用意思是名词"舞台",这里作动词表示"上演"。

(4) She was the first dancer who learned from Western dances in modern China.

- 她是现代中国第一个学习西方舞蹈的舞者。

- who learned from Western dances in modern China 是 who 作引导词的定语从句,修饰 the first dancer。

■ Passage B ■

◆ Important Words ◆

ballet [ˈbæleɪ] *n.* a theatrical representation of a story that is performed to music by trained dancers 芭蕾舞

e.g. 1. She was resolved to become a ballet dancer.

2. My niece has practiced ballet for six years.

empire [ˈempaɪə(r)] *n.* a group of countries that are all controlled by one ruler or government 帝国

e.g. 1. She once ruled over a vast empire.

2. At that time, the Roman Empire had already decayed.

impress [ɪmˈpres] *vt.* to make someone feel admiration and respect 使……有印象, 影响

e.g. 1. His words are strongly impressed on my memory.

2. She impressed me as a hard worker.

breathtaking['breθ₁teɪkɪŋ] *a.* very impressive, exciting, or surprising 令人赞叹的,惊人的

e. g.　1. The beauty of the sunrise is really breathtaking.

　　　　2. The prospect from the balcony was breathtaking.

overcome[₁əʊvə'kʌm] *vt.* to successfully control a feeling or problem that prevents you from achieving sth 战胜,克服

e. g.　1. He is consciously trying to overcome his weakness.

　　　　2. Love makes him overcome the sense of isolation and separateness, yet it permits to be himself, to retain his integrity.

throughout[θruː'aʊt] *prep.* during all of a particular period, from the beginning to the end 自始自终,遍及

e. g.　1. Throughout most of human history, mathematics and physics have been inseparably joined.

　　　　2. Throughout the last fifteen years, she'd been my closest friend, sharing my joy and sadness.

legend['ledʒənd] *n.* an old, well known story, often about brave people, adventures, or magical events 传说,传奇故事

e. g.　1. The musician made the legend into a beautiful ballad.

　　　　2. Anyone familiar with the legend of Robin Hood knows archery competitions date back at least to mediaeval times.

become famous for 因……闻名

e. g.　1. Spain used to become famous for its strong armada.

　　　　2. The heroine became famous for the courage and daring action.

succeed in 成功;有成就

e. g.　1. He succeeded in getting a place at art school.

　　　　2. If you study hard, you will succeed in the examination.

◆Explanation of Difficult Sentences◆

(1)... and the following year she succeeded in many roles formerly danced by the famed British ballet dancer Alicia Markova.

● 翌年,她成功地扮演了多个以前由英国著名芭蕾舞蹈家艾丽西亚·玛尔科娃担当的角色。

- 本句中过去分词短语 formerly danced by the famed British ballet dancer Alicia Markova 作后置定语修饰前面的 many roles。

(2) In the 1960's she was teamed with the Russian ballet dancer, Rudolf Nureyev, at the Royal Ballet in England.

- 在 20 世纪 60 年代,她在英国皇家芭蕾舞团与俄罗斯芭蕾舞蹈家鲁道夫·纽瑞耶夫搭档。
- Rudolf Nureyev 为插入语,这里是说话者对所表达意思的补充、解释。插入语位置灵活,常常用逗号或破折号与其他成分隔开,并且在语法上不影响其他成分。

(3) What impresses audience most about Margot Fonteyn was her incredible and breathtaking dancing.

- 玛戈·芳婷给观众留下最深印象的是她令人难以置信和激动人心的舞蹈。
- What impresses audience most about Margot Fonteyn 是主语从句。主语从句是在复合句中充当主语的从句。

(4) Her art brought pleasure to many people who saw her dance.

- 她的艺术给许多观看表演的人带来欢乐。
- who saw her dance 作定语从句修饰 many people。

(5) She overcame bad feet that would have stopped most people, but she could light up the stage like no other dancer could.

- 她战胜了会让大多数人放弃(舞台表演)的脚伤。但她可以照亮整个舞台,那是其他舞者都难以企及的。
- bad feet that would have stopped most people 是 that 作引导词的定语从句。that 在从句中充当主语。注意和同位语从句的区分,同位语从句中的引导词在从句中只起连接作用,不作任何句子成分。

IV. Keys, Tapescripts and Text Translations

■ Keys ■

◆ Lead-in ◆

1. Margot Fonteyn.
2. Open.

◆ Module 1 Learn to Talk ◆

Past Events and Experience

1. *Listen to the dialogue between the dancer Steve and his friend. As you listen, underline expressions of talking about past events.*

Eric: Say, Steve. ...

Steve: Yeah?

Eric: Did you take Alice as your partner before you went to the States?

Steve: Oh, yeah, I did.

Eric: How did you feel when you met her first?

Steve: Uh... I remember it very clearly. That was in the Paris Dancing College. One day I saw Alice dancing in a classroom by accident. She was charming, beautiful, and really special! So then I thought she was a perfect partner for my dance performance.

Eric: Yeah. And what happened next?

Steve: I soon went to know her and we took part in the Argentina Tango Programme together.

Eric: What did both of you do after that?

Steve: Uh, we participated in the national dance competition in France.

Eric: Were you nervous when you danced at that time?

Steve: Yeah, very nervous but also excited. You know, we won the first prize finally.

Eric: That's terrific!

2. Open.

3. *Listen to a short passage. Number the following sentences from 1 to 5 according to the time sequence.*

④After six months, I couldn't see the value in it.

⑤The minute I dropped out I could stop taking the required classes that didn't interest me.

①My biological mother decided to put me up for adoption.

③17 years later I did go to college.

②My parents, who were on a waiting list, got a call in the middle of the night.

4. Open.   5. Open.

Stories of Dancers

Before You Listen

1. Open.   2. Open.

While You Listen

1. *Listen and answer the questions about the two dancers Isadora Duncan and Martha Graham. Check (√) the correct box.*

Who...	Duncan	Graham
(1) was born in California?	√	□
(2) thought dancing should be an art?	√	□
(3) created "Chronicle"?	□	√
(4) did not like ballet?	√	□

续表

Who…	Duncan	Graham
(5) established the dance programme in New York City?	□	√
(6) made a speech in Berlin in 1903?	√	□
(7) died in 1991?	□	√
(8) received award of the Presidential Medal of Freedom?	□	√

2. *Listen again and fill in the following table about the artistic features of Isadora Duncan and Martha Graham.*

	Artistic features
Duncan	(1) She wanted to live by her own rules, not by what other people thought was right or wrong. (2) She wanted her "modern" dance style to be free and natural. (3) The movement of the waves, of the winds, of the earth is ever in the same lasting harmony.
Graham	(1) The dance expressed sadness and loneliness. (2) Graham's dances were powerful, with strong and sharp movements.

After You Listen

Open.

◆ Module 2   Learn to Read ◆

Warm-up

1. (1) Yu Rongling.
   (2) Open.
2. Open.

Passage A   First Dancer of Modern China: Yu Rongling

Reading Comprehension

1. *Global understanding*
   (1) The passage mainly introduces Yu Rongling, the first dancer of modern China, including her life and dance learning experience.
   (2) When she traveled abroad with her father, She learned dance in Japan and then in France.
2. *Detailed understanding*
   (1) A (2) D (3) C (4) A (5) C

Language Practice

1. Open.
2. *Make sure you know the words in the table below. Choose the word or phrase to complete each of the*

following sentences. Change the form where necessary.

(1) nominated (2) ambassador (3) persuade (4) achievement

(5) feudal (6) Dynasty (7) performance

3. *Translate the following sentences，paying special attention to the coloured parts.*

(1) 官方价格体系通常对此反应迟钝。

市长是选举产生的官员。

(2) 做母亲的不应过分偏爱某一个孩子。

我们喜欢那个老师。

(3) 一些女孩在舞台上跳舞。

我们会在 3 年内举办 100 场演出。

(4) 法庭判他有罪。

他因与犯罪分子鬼混而招致灾祸。

(5) 音乐家正在忙于为皇家婚礼谱写仪式乐曲。

今晚王室成员将出席音乐会。

(6) 她师从当时在巴黎演出和教学的美国著名舞蹈家伊莎多拉·邓肯。

(7) 她的父亲不容许自己的女儿成为舞蹈演员，在当时这被看作是低贱的职业。

Passage B   Dancing Queen

Warm-up Questions

She was an incredible, disciplined, and receptible girl.

Reading Comprehension

1. *Global understanding*

Paragraph 1：c   Paragraph 2：a   Paragraph 3：b

2. *Detailed understanding*

(1) B   (2) A   (3) C   (4) D

3. *Information matching*

TimeTime	Things that happened to Fonteyn
(1) In 1919	Margot Fonteyn was born in Reigate, Surrey, England.
In 1934	(2) She joined Sadler's Wells Ballet, which is now the Royal Ballet.
(3) By 1940	She was their principal dancer.
In 1956	(4) Margot received the honorary title of Dame Commander of the British Empire.
In 1991	(5) Margot Fonteyn died.

Language Practice

1. *Translate the coloured phrases in the following pairs of sentences. Pay attention to how the same*

word can have different meanings.

(1) light up

他<u>点燃</u>了一支香烟。

太阳<u>照亮</u>了天空和大地。

(2) live on

这些传统将世代<u>相传</u>。

那个老人靠他女儿的收入<u>维持生活</u>。

(3) look up to

学生们都很<u>尊敬</u>那位哲学老教授。

小女孩个子太矮,只好<u>仰着头</u>看她的妹妹。

2. *Complete the following sentences by translating into English the Chinese given in brackets.*

(1) was said to be born in a small village.

(2) these obstacles he/she must overcome.

(3) impressed foreign tourists.

(4) tends to raise the price to a more reasonable level.

(5) He had succeeded to his father's estate.

(6) schools were opened throughout the country.

◆Module 3　Culture Link◆

1. Open.

2. *Can you tell people's thoughts or feelings by looking at their body language? Study the following cases and match them with the correct meaning from the box below.*

(1)—(5) c a b e d

■■■■■■■ Tapescripts ■■■■■■■

◆Module 1　Learn to Talk◆

Past Events and Experience

3. *Listen to a short passage. Number the following sentences from 1 to 5 according to the time sequence.*

The first story is about connecting the dots. It started before I was born. My biological mother was a young, unwed college graduate student, and she decided to put me up for adoption. So my parents, who were on a waiting list, got a call in the middle of the night asking: "We have an unexpected baby boy; do you want him?" They said: "Of course."

And 17 years later I did go to college. But I naively chose a college that was almost as expensive as Stanford, and all of my working-class parents' savings were being spent on my college tuition. After six months, I couldn't see the value in it. I had no idea what I wanted to do with my life and no idea how college was going to help me figure it out. So I decided to drop out and trust that it would all work out OK. It was pretty scary at the time, but looking back it was one of the best deci-sions I ever made. The minute I dropped out I could stop taking the required classes that didn't in-terest me, and begin dropping in on the ones that looked interesting.

5. *Listen to the beginning of "My Grandma's Story" below and try to tell the whole story in front of class.*

I love listening to my great-grandma's stories, so I didn't object when she started to tell me a story about one of her strange experiences over a glass of iced tea... My Great-Great Granddad died in 1918 at the age of 48 when he fell off of a galloping horse. My Great Grandma was only 17 when this happened. The story goes that at the get-together after the funeral, a strange man showed up. No one had seen him at the funeral, or anytime else for that matter. He stayed for a long time, hardly talking to anybody, and refusing to take off his coat and hat...

Stories of Musicians

Barefoot dancer

Angela Isadora Duncan was born in San Francisco, California in 1877. She wanted to make dancing her life's work, and she wanted to live by her own rules, not by what other people thought was right or wrong. The kind of dancing Isadora wanted to do was new and different from other dances at the time. She thought dancing should be an art, not just entertainment.

Isadora Duncan did not like ballet. She said that ballet dancers had too many rules to follow about how they should stand and bend and move. She said ballet was "ugly and against nature." She wanted her "modern" dance style to be free and natural. Isadora liked to move her arms and legs in very smooth motions. She said this was like waves in the ocean, or trees swaying in the wind.

In 1903, when she was twenty-six, she made a famous speech in Berlin. She said: "Nature is the source of dance. The movement of the waves, of the winds, of the earth is ever in the same last-ing harmony... Every creature moves according to its nature... that is according to its feelings and physical structure."

The famous American poet Carl Sandburg wrote this about Isadora Duncan: "The wind? I am the wind. The sea and the moon? I am the sea and the moon. Tears, pain, love, bird-flights? I am all of them. I dance what I am. Sin, prayer, flight, the light that never was on land or sea? I dance what I am."

The Mother of Modern Dance

Martha Graham was born in the small town of Allegheny, Pennsylvania, in eighteen ninety-four. After Martha turned fourteen years old, her family moved to Santa Barbara, California.

In 1936, Graham created "Chronicle", one of her most important dances. "Chronicle" was influenced by current events including the Great Depression and the Spanish Civil War. The dance expressed sadness and loneliness.

At first, people did not react well to Graham's style of dancing. It was very different from European ballet, which was more commonly accepted. Graham's dances were powerful, with strong and sharp movements. These movements are still used in modern dance today.

In 1951, Graham was among the people who established the dance program at the Juilliard School in New York City. It is still one of the best arts schools in the country. Many famous artists have begun their careers by studying there.

Martha Graham received many awards during her lifetime, including the Presidential Medal of Freedom in 1976. She was the first dancer to receive the country's highest civilian honour. She died in 1991 at the age of 96. In 1998, Time magazine listed her as the "Dancer of the Century" and as one of the most important people of the twentieth century.

◆Module 2　Learn to Read◆

Warm-up（Passage B）

She was a very receptible little girl, of course. And very intelligent. The intelligence is never obvious. Because she was a very natural person. She had hundreds of friends, good time in life, enjoyed everything. But she had with an amazing way applying herself to know, even at that age. But I found her, the most incredibly, disciplined, receptible child I have ever worked with. And I think all choreographers had the same thing to say about her, marvelous.

◆Module 3　Culture Link◆

This is a world where what we say is all important. "They said this day will never come…" We hang on every word. "Tomorrow we begin again. Thank you." But are we getting all the message? "Older, darker, mean, psychopath, serial killer…" Research had shown just 7 percent of human communication is through the actual words. "93 percent of what we communicate with other is non-verbal. 93 percent, think about that, 93 percent. So, it's our tone of voice, our pitch, our posture, micro expression on our face in different gestures that we might use. So we put on significance on 7 percent for words. We shouldn't really be doing that." Beyond the words lies a fascinating world of non-verbal communication. The secret world of body language…

President Clinton had a more serious problem when rumors of his personal relationship with Monica Lewinsky began to circulate. He decided to make a very public televise denial. His words were crystal clear. "And I work on to pray late last night. But I want to say one thing to the American people." Clinton was addressing both the TV Audience and reporters of the White House. "I did not have sexual relations with that woman. Miss Lewinsky." But his normally assure body language was not conveying a reassuring message. "These allegations are false. And I need go back to work for the

American people. Thank you. " "To show you're integrity. Your face, your head, your gestures and your body need to be in alignment. In this case, he's gesturing in one direction, and looking into another direction. " "I did not have sexual relations with that woman. " "So he's pointing here, but looking here. Well, that is a disconnect. That doesn't make sense why there is inconsistency. It should be America I want to tell you something. Not America I want to tell you something. " Now, look again the way the president's head move. "I never told anybody to lie. Not a single time. Never. " "Never, never never. Not a single time. We see the head shaking no. But we didn't see his head shaking no when he say he didn't have sexual relationship with that woman…"

We pay so much attention to the words people speak, "I earn everything I got" But remember 93 percent of human communication is delivered through body language. "When there's a conflict between the words and the body language. I always believe the body language. " Read body language accurately and you look at the world through new eyes.

■ Text Translations ■

◆ Passage A ◆

现代中国第一舞者：裕容龄

裕容龄（1882—1973）是中国晚清官员的女儿。她把西方舞蹈引入了中国。

1895 年裕容龄的父亲成为驻日公使，她随父亲去了国外。在日本居住期间，裕容龄学习日本古典舞蹈。四年后，她的父亲被任命为法国大使，她又随父亲去了法国。

在巴黎，她师从当时在巴黎演出和教学的美国著名舞蹈家伊莎多拉·邓肯。三年后，邓肯非常满意裕容龄的表现，邀请她在其舞剧中担任角色。

然而，裕容龄生在一个封建家庭。她的父亲不容许自己的女儿成为舞蹈演员，在当时这被看作低贱的职业。但是裕容龄很坚决，她勇敢面对父亲并最终说服了他。后来裕容龄在巴黎音乐学院进一步深造并参加了更多的舞台表演。

1903 年裕容龄回到中国开始向中国介绍西方的舞蹈。她在宫廷里表演舞蹈，深受慈禧太后喜爱。之后，她在西方舞蹈的实践中进行了自己的创作。中华人民共和国成立后，裕容龄被国务院任命为艺术官员。

裕容龄逝世于 1973 年。她是现代中国第一个学习西方舞蹈的舞者。

◆ Passage B ◆

舞蹈皇后

玛戈·芳婷出生于英国萨里郡的赖盖特，是世界上最伟大的芭蕾舞蹈家之一。她因在《睡美人》《天鹅湖》《吉赛尔》中的表演而成名。最初她在中国学习芭蕾。1934 年她加入圣德勒·威尔士芭蕾舞舞团，也就是现在的皇家芭蕾舞团。翌年，她成功扮演了以前由英国著名芭蕾舞蹈家艾丽西亚·玛尔科娃扮演的舞蹈角色。直到 1940 年，她都一直是该团的首席舞者。1956 年玛戈·芳婷获得大英帝国"女爵士"荣誉称号。20 世纪 60 年代，她在英国皇家芭蕾舞团与俄罗斯芭蕾舞蹈家鲁道夫·纽瑞耶夫搭档。

玛戈·芳婷给观众留下最深印象的是她令人难以置信和激动人心的舞蹈。她的艺术给许多观看表演的人带来欢乐。她让他们看到芭蕾可以是什么样子并将其提升到一个更高的水平。她的舞蹈给世界带来了更多的美，让所有年轻舞者为之倾倒。

　　玛戈·芳婷比很多人都用功。她战胜了会让大多数人放弃(舞台表演)的脚伤。她可以照亮整个舞台,那是其他舞者难以企及的。她终其一生都在努力完善自己的艺术。玛戈·芳婷不幸于1991年去世,但她的传奇故事将一直流传下去。

Unit 5　Designers

I. Background Information

1. Designer: A designer is a person who designs. More formally, a designer is an agent that "specifies the structural properties of a design object". In practice, anyone who creates tangible or intangible objects, such as consumer products, processes, laws, games and graphics, is referred to as a designer.

2. Classical areas of design: Classically, the main areas of design were only Painting, Sculpture and Architecture, which were understood as the major arts. The design of clothing, furniture and other common artifacts were left mostly to tradition or artisans specializing in hand making them.

3. Subdivision of classical areas of design: With the increasing complexity of today's society, and due to the needs of mass production where more time is usually associated with more cost, the production methods became more complex and with them the way designs and their production is created. The classical areas are now subdivided in smaller and more specialized domains of design according to the product designed or perhaps its means of production.

◆ Architecture is both the process and product of planning, designing and constructing form, space and ambience that reflect functional, technical, social, and aesthetic considerations. It requires the creative manipulation and coordination of material, technology, light and shadow. Architecture also encompasses the pragmatic aspects of realizing buildings and structures, including scheduling, cost estimating and construction administration. As documentation produced by architects, typically drawings, plans and technical specifications, architecture defines the structure and/or behavior of a building or any other kind of system that is to be or has been constructed.

◆ Engineering is the discipline, art, and profession of acquiring and applying scientific, mathematical, economic, social, and practical knowledge to design and build structures, machines, devices, systems, materials and processes that safely realize improvements to the lives of people.

◆ Landscape design is an independent profession and a design and art tradition, practiced by landscape designers, combining nature and culture. In contemporary practice landscape design bridges between landscape architecture and garden design.

◆ Urban Design concerns the arrangement, appearance and functionality of towns and cities, and in particular the shaping and uses of urban public space. It has traditionally been regarded as a disciplinary subset of urban planning, landscape architecture, or architecture and in more recent times has been linked to emergent disciplines such as landscape urbanism. However, with its increasing prominence in the activities of these disciplines, it is better conceptualised as a design practice that operates at the intersection of all three, and requires a good understanding of a range of others besides, such as real estate development, urban economics, political economy and social theory.

◆ Interior Design is a multi-faceted profession in which creative and technical solutions are applied within a structure to achieve a built interior environment and home lifestyle enhancement.

◆ Furniture Design is the mass noun for the movable objects intended to support various human activities such as seating and sleeping in beds, to hold objects at a convenient height for work using horizontal surfaces above the ground, or to store things. Storage furniture such as a nightstand often makes use of doors, drawers, shelves and locks to contain, organize or secure smaller objects such as clothes, tools, books, and household goods.

◆ Industrial Design is a combination of applied art and applied science, whereby the aesthetics, ergonomics and usability of products may be improved for marketability and production. The role of an industrial designer is to create and execute design solutions towards problems of form, usability, physical ergonomics, marketing, brand development and sales.

◆ Packaging Design is the science, art, and technology of enclosing or protecting products for distribution, storage, sale, and use. Packaging also refers to the process of design, evaluation, and production of packages.

◆ Fashion Design is the art of the application of design and aesthetics or natural beauty to clothing and accessories. Fashion design is influenced by cultural and social attitudes, and has varied over time and place.

◆ Jewelry Design is the art or professional of creating, crafting, fabricating, or rendering designs for jewelry. This is an ancient practice of the goldsmith or metalworker that evolved to a billion-dollar industry with the odyssey from ancient cultures into the machine age. Jewelry design falls under the category of what is commonly known as "functional art", being art that can be worn or used.

◆ Game Design a subset of game development, is the process of designing the content and rules of a game in the pre-production stage and design of game-play, environment, and storyline, characters during production stage. The term is also used to describe both the game design embodied in a game as well as documentation that describes such a design. Game design requires artistic and technical competence as well as writing skills.

II. Notes

1. Notes to Lead-in

苏州博物馆新馆简介:苏州博物馆新馆位于苏州老城东北街和齐门路相交的东北角,占地面积 10 700 平方米、建筑面积 19 000 余平方米,2006 年 10 月竣工开馆,设计者为著名的建筑设计大师贝聿铭。该博物管是全国重点文物保护单位。

苏州博物馆新馆建筑群座北朝南,被分成三大块:中央部分为入口、前庭、中央大厅和主庭院;西部为博物馆主展区;东部为次展区和行政办公区。这种以中轴线对称的东、中、西三路布局和新馆东侧的忠王府格局相互印衬,十分和谐。

在新馆建筑的构造上,玻璃、开放式钢结构让现代人可以在室内借到大片天光,屋面形态的设计突破了中国传统建筑"大屋顶"在采光方面的束缚。室内设计部分,包括陈列展览设计均经贝聿铭本人审定,以保证内外风格和所有功能的协调统一。新馆不仅有建筑的创新,还有园艺的创新,新馆园林造景设计是在传统风景园林的精髓中提炼而出的,由池塘、假山、小桥、亭台、竹林等古典园林元素组成的现代风格的山水园,与传统园林有机结合,成为一代名园拙政园在当今的创造性延续。

2. Notes to Module 1

(1) Fashion show

时装表演是由时装模特在特定场所通过走台表演、展示时装的活动。一般是在铺有长长的跑道式地毯的表演台上,模特穿上特制的时装和配以相应的饰品,以特定的步伐和节奏来回走动并做出各种动作和造型。时装模特是传递设计师意图的使者,用自己的形体姿态动作与时装融合,使服装、音乐、表演融为一体,达到高度完美的艺术统一。

(2) Fengshui

风水本为相地之术,即临场校察地理的方法,也叫地相,古称堪舆术。相传风水的创始人是九天玄女,比较完善的风水学问起源于战国时代。风水的核心思想是人与大自然的和谐。早期的风水主要关乎宫殿、住宅、村落、墓地的选址、座向、建设等方法及原则,原意是选择合适的地方的一门学问。

中国风水学或者叫堪舆学,现称居住环境学,起源于原始时期,雏形于尧舜时期,成熟于汉唐时期,鼎盛于明清时期。风水学是人类在长期的居住实践中积累的宝贵经验。朝阳光、避风雨、防火灾、近水源、利出行成了最基本的居住理论。几千年甚至几万年来人们不断地总结居住环境的优劣,到了汉唐时期就形成了很成熟很系统的中国风水学理论。彭祖弟子青衣说:"内气萌生,外气成形,内外相乘,风水自成"。晋人郭璞《葬经》解释风水:"气乘风则散,界水则止,古人聚之使不散,行之使有止,故谓之风水。"汉朝淮南王所著《淮南子》论述道:"天地运行之道。至月令有阴阳变化,有相冲克之时,有相合之时,前者凶,后者吉。盖堪舆之义实为天地之道也。"许慎《说文》解释:"堪,天道;舆,地道。"

(3) The Bank of China in Hong Kong

中银大厦。香港中国银行大厦,由贝聿铭建筑师事务所设计,1990 年完工。总建筑面积12.9 万平方米,地上 70 层,楼高 315 米,加顶上两杆的高度共有 367.4 米。建成时是香港最高的建筑物,亦是美国地区以外最高的摩天大厦。结构采用 4 角 12 层高的巨形钢柱支撑,室内无一根柱子。仔细观察中银大厦,会发现许多贝氏作品惯用的设计,以平面为例,中银大厦是一个正方平面,对角划成 4 组三角形,每组三角形的高度不同,节节高升,使得各个立面在严谨的几何规范内变化多端。至于平面的概念,可以溯至 1973 年的马德里大厦,马德里大厦亦是以方正的正面做多边的分割;分析其组合,乃系两个平等四边形的变化。中银大厦外型像竹子的"节节高升",象征着力量、生机、茁壮和锐意进取的精神;基座的麻石外墙代表长城,代表中国。

(4) Glasgow

格拉斯哥。苏格兰第一大城与第一大商港,英国第三大城市。位于苏格兰西部的克莱德河(R. Clyde)河口。行政上,格拉斯哥属于格拉斯哥市(City of Glasgow)的管辖范围,是苏格兰 32 个一级行政区(称为统一管理区)底下的一个,长年以来一直是英国工党的执政领域。

(5) Edinburgh

爱丁堡,英国北部城市,苏格兰首府,经济和文化中心。在苏格兰中部低地、福斯湾的南岸,面积 260 平方公里。1329 年建市,1437—1707 年为苏格兰王国首都。爱丁堡的造纸和印刷出版业历史悠久,造船、化工、核能、电子、电缆、玻璃和食品等工业也占重要地位。随着北海油田的开发,又建立一系列相关工业与服务业。爱丁保还是重要的运输枢纽、航空港。城东北临福斯湾的利斯为其外港,是福斯湾港区大港口之一。爱丁堡是一座文化古城,18 世纪时为欧洲文化、艺术、哲学和科学中心,在这里有 1583 年建立的爱丁堡大学,还有古城堡、大教堂、宫殿、艺术陈列馆等名胜古迹。

(6)Buddhism

佛教,世界三大宗教之一,由公元前 6 世纪古印度的迦毗罗卫国(今尼泊尔境内)王子所创,他的名字是悉达多·乔达摩,因为他属于释迦(Sākya)族,人们又称他为释迦牟尼,意思是释迦族的圣人。佛教广泛流传于亚洲的许多国家,西汉末年经丝绸之路传入我国。

(7)Jaguar

捷豹汽车,最具有英国特色的豪华汽车。公司前身诞生于 1922 年,在 1935 年正式推出 JAGUAR 汽车。从推出到今天 JAGUAR 始终以其优雅迷人的设计和卓越不凡的技术引领着豪华车市场的新潮流,成为了代表时尚的奢华标志,并借此在全球吸引了无数的追随者。捷豹汽车有"英国骑士"之称,是有 80 余年历史的世界一流名车品牌。让其闻名于世的是跑车、赛车和高档轿车。

(8)Ford

福特汽车公司,世界最大的汽车企业之一。1903 年,亨利·福特(Henry Ford)于美国底特律市创建福特汽车公司,公司名称取自创始人亨利·福特(Henry Ford)的姓氏。公司现任首席执行官为艾伦·穆拉利,总部设在美国密执安州迪尔伯恩市。

3. Notes to Module 2

(1)The John Fitzgerald Kennedy Library

肯尼迪图书馆。1964 年为纪念已故美国总统约翰·肯尼迪,决定在波士顿港口建造一座永久性建筑物——约翰·肯尼迪图书馆。这座建造了 15 年之久,于 1979 年落成的图书馆,由于设计新颖、造型大胆、技术高超,在美国建筑界引起轰动,公认是美国建筑史上最佳杰作之一。美国建筑界宣布 1979 年是"贝聿铭年",授予他该年度的美国建筑学院金质奖章。

(2)The Fragrant Hill Hotel

香山饭店。香山饭店是由国际著名美籍华裔建筑设计师贝聿铭先生主持设计的一座融中国古典建筑艺术、香山饭店园林艺术、环境艺术为一体的四星级酒店。饭店位于北京西山风景区的香山公园内,坐拥自然美景,四时景色各异。饭店建筑独具特色,1984 年曾获美国建筑学会荣誉奖。

(3)The East Building of the National Gallery of Art, Washington, D.C.

华盛顿国家艺术馆东馆由世界级建筑大师贝聿铭设计,1978 年建造成功,当时的美国总统卡特在东馆的开幕仪式上称,"它不但是华盛顿市和谐而周全的一部分,而且是公众生活与艺术情趣之间日益增强联系的象征。"称贝聿铭是"不可多得的杰出建筑师"。东馆的地理位置十分显要。它东望国会大厦,西望白宫。而它所占有的地形却是使建筑师们颇难处理的不规则四边形。为了使这座建筑物能够同周围环境构成高度协调的景色,贝聿铭精心构思,创造性地把不同高度,不同形状的平台、楼梯、斜坡和廊柱交错相连,给人以变幻莫测的感觉。阳光透过蜘蛛网似的天窗,从不同的角度射入,自成一幅美丽的图画。这座费时十年,耗资近亿美元建成的东馆,被誉为"现代艺术与建筑充满创意的结合"。

(4) Louis Vuitton

　　路易威登成立于 1854 年,第一代创始人是 19 世纪一位法国巴黎专门为王室贵族打造旅行行李箱包的技师路易·威登,他制作的皮箱技术精良,在当时的巴黎名气非常响亮,因此,逐渐地,路易威登成为皮制旅行用品最精致的象征。如果要买高级的皮件,当以路易威登为首选,尤其是皮制的旅行箱更是许多有钱的绅士贵妇不可缺少的。路易威登的皮件精品可列为顶级名牌皮件商品之一。路易威登的精品并不只有皮件,它还有各式皮包、男女装、丝巾、钢笔、手表等。全世界公认最顶级的品牌 Louis Vuitton,百年来一直以四瓣花跟路易威登的缩写组合,成为各时代潮流的领导者,路易威登历经时代的转变,不仅没有呈现老态还不断地登峰造极。

4. Notes to Module 3

　　迷信(Superstition):认识是有限的,而且相当有限。当人面对巨大的未知的空间的时候,往往会提出自己的解释。迷信是指人们对于事物盲目地信仰或崇拜。狭义的迷信,按照我国解放以后约定俗成的习惯,是专指人们信星占、卜巫、风水、命相和神鬼等的思想和行为。迷信本身并不是与科学对立的认识体系,而是一种对事物错误认识的思维方式。迷信的更多含义倾向于"盲目的相信、不理解的相信。"

III. Language Points

▰ Passage A ▰

◆ Important Words ◆

architect [ˈɑːkɪtekt] *n*. a person who designs buildings and advises in their construction 建筑师;a person who is responsible for planning or creating an idea, an event or a situation 设计师

e.g　1. The new building was built from the design of a famous architect.

　　　2. Every man is the architect of his own fortune.

construction [kənˈstrʌkʃn] *n*. the process, art, or manner of constructing sth; a thing constructed 建筑;建筑物

e.g.　1. There are two new hotels under construction.

　　　2. The building is a peculiarly shaped construction.

project [prɒˈdʒekt] *n*. a planned piece of work that is designed to find information about sth, to produce sth new, or to improve sth 规划;计划;项目

e.g.　1. a project to build a new road.

　　　2. In the meeting, they are doing a special project on a new plant.

renovation [renəˈveɪʃn] *n*. the act of improving and restoring, the state of being restored to its former good condition 翻新;修复;整修

e.g.　1. The building was closed for renovation.

　　　2. Older churches underwent major renovations.

soothe [suːð] *vt.* to bring comfort, solace, or reassurance to 安慰；使平静；to make (pains, aches) less sharp or severe 使(痛苦、疼痛)缓和；减轻

e. g.　1. I've managed to soothe him down a bit.

　　　 2. This medicine should soothe your aching tooth.

estimate [ˈestɪmeɪt] *vt.* to judge tentatively or approximately the value, worth, or significance of 估计，估价

e. g.　1. They estimated the distance at about three miles.

　　　 2. The cost of the project has been estimated at about 10 million dollars.

ease [iːz] *vt.* to give relief to (the body or mind from pain, discomfort, anxiety, etc.) 缓和；改善

e. g.　1. The pain began to ease.

　　　 2. The tension between the two groups has eased off.

lay out 设计；安排；布置

e. g　1. The architect laid out the interior of the building.

　　　 2. All the terms are laid out in the contract.

take on 决定做；同意负责；承担

e. g.　1. You need to take on your responsibilities.

　　　 2. I can't take on any extra work.

◆ Explanation of Difficult Sentences ◆

(1) One of these was the renovation of the Louvre Museum, which Pei was asked to join.

● 其中一项就是整修卢浮宫博物馆,贝聿铭应邀参与这项工程。

● 句中的 these 指前面提到的 construction projects,该句 which 引导的是一个非限制性定语从句,修饰前面提到的 one of these。

(2) One of Pei's designs was the glass and steel pyramid which served as the entrance to the Louvre, …

● 贝聿铭的设计方案是在卢浮宫建一个玻璃和钢架结构的金字塔,这个玻璃金字塔就是卢浮宫博物馆的入口……

● 该句中 which 引导的是一个限制性定语从句,修饰前面的 the glass and steel pyramid。

(3) … because many people felt that the glass and steel pyramid looked quite out of place in front of the Louvre Museum with its classical architecture.

- 因为,许多人认为这个玻璃和钢结构的金字塔与具有传统设计风格的卢浮宫博物馆看起来格格不入。
- 该句 many people felt 后面带了一个宾语从句由 that 引导,宾语从句中介词短语 with its classical architecture 说明它前面名词的特征或性质。

■ **Passage B** ■

◆**Important Words**◆

refer[rɪ'fɜː(r)]*vi.* to speak of or mention about sb/sth 指;提到;提及;to send, take, hand over (to sb or sth)for help, advice or a decision 送交;提交(某人或机构)以处理或决定(与 to 连用)

e. g. 1. Don't refer to the matter again.

　　　2. He referred the case to the High Court.

fashion['fæʃn]*n.* social standing or prominence especially as signalized by dress or conduct 流行款式;时尚款式;时装

e. g. 1. Is it the fashion to wear short skirts?

　　　2. She was dressed in the latest fashion.

odd[ɒd]*a.* not regular, expected, or planned 临时的;不固定的 differing markedly from the usual or ordinary or accepted 奇怪的; 古怪的

e. g. 1. He makes a living by doing odd job.

　　　2. I had rather an odd experience the other day.

appoint[ə'pɔɪnt]*vt.* to pick (someone) by one's authority for a specific position or duty 任命,委派;to decide upon (the time or date for an event) usually from a position of authority 确定, 指定;约定

e. g. 1. He was appointed secretary.

　　　2. We must appoint a day to meet again.

campaign[kæm'peɪn]*n.* a connected series of operations designed to bring about a particular result 运动;a connected series of military operations forming a distinct phase of a war 战役

e. g. 1. The university is organizing a campaign to attract a more diverse student population.

　　　2. The army set off on campaign.

strategy['strætədʒi]*n.* a method worked out in advance for achieving some objectives 战略,策略;the means or procedure for doing sth 策略,计谋

e. g. 1. They worked out a strategy to raise students' achievement test scores over the next three years.

　　　2. You'll need a better strategy than just knocking on doors if you want to sell that many magazines.

distribution[ˌdɪstrɪˈbjuːʃn]*n.* the action or process of supplying goods to stores and other businesses that sell to consumers; the action of sharing sth out among a number of recipients 销售；分发；分配

e. g.　1．They have to carefully distribute the school's limited scholarship money so that it benefits more students.

　　　 2．These books are distributed freely.

recognized[ˈrekəɡnaɪzd]*a.* being thought of as very good or important by people in general 公认的；经过验证的

e. g.　1．She's a recognized authority on the subject.

　　　 2．The University offers many courses that lead to recognized qualifications.

prestige[presˈtiːʒ]*n.* standing or estimation in the eyes of people 威信，威望，声望；commanding position in people's minds 地位

e. g.　1．The contract will affect our national prestige in the world.

　　　 2．The job has low pay and low prestige.

◆Explanation of Difficult Sentences◆

(1) Through such experience, Louis Vuitton developed advanced knowledge of what made for a good luggage.

- 这些经历使路易·威登积累了先进的箱包制作知识。
- 句中 develop 是"发展，逐渐形成"的意思，of 后面是一个由 what 引导的宾语从句，句子中 make 是"生产，制造"的意思。

(2) It was then that he began to design his own luggage, which set the foundation for LV Company.

- 此时，他开始了自己的箱包设计，这为 LV 公司的建立打下了基础。
- 该句中 which 引导的是一个非限制性定语从句，修饰前面整个句子。

(3) Today, the company markets its product through its own stores located throughout the world.

- 如今，公司通过分布在世界各地自己的商店来销售产品。
- 该句中 market 是动词，意为"出售，推销"，located throughout the world 是过去分词短语做定语，修饰它前面的名词 stores。

(4) Louis Vuitton has no discount sales, nor does it have any duty-free stores.

- 路易威登产品不打折，公司也不开免税商店。
- 该句中否定副词 nor 引导的句子需要倒装。

IV. Keys, Tapescripts and Text Translations

■ Keys ■

◆ Lead-in ◆

1. Open.
2. (1) Ieoh Ming Pei.

   (2) It started in 2002, and was inaugurated on October 6, 2006.

   (3) 2,200 square meters.

   (4) 247.

◆ Module 1　Learn to Talk ◆

Giving Opinions

1. *Linda and her mother are talking about a fashion show. Listen to the model dialogue, and underline the expressions of giving opinions.*

   Linda: Mom, look at this fashion show. Does that miniskirt look good on me?

   Mother: I don't think it's suitable for a student like you.

   Linda: No, you are out-dated. It's very fashionable.

   Mother: I don't agree. What's the point of following the fashion?

   Linda: I believe if you don't follow the fashion trends, you'll be looked down upon.

   Mother: It's too short.

   Linda: Yeah, I think so. But it can well display my legs.

   Mother: You are probably right, but I still feel young students need to spend more time on study and less on fashion.

   Linda: Perhaps.

2. Open.
3. *Listen to a conversation and fill in the blanks with the information you hear.*

   (1) world-class　(2) Hong Kong and Shanghai　(3) in China　(4) knife

4. Open.

Stories of Designers and Their Works

Before You Listen

1. Open.　2. Open.

While You Listen

1. *Listen to a short passage about the problem of Fengshui in architecture and decide whether the following statements are true (T) or false (F).*

   (1) T　(2) T　(3) T　(4) T　(5) T

2. *Listen to an interview with the car designer Ian Callum and fill in the blanks with the information you hear.*

(1) only　(2) American　(3) expressive　(4) low

After You Listen
Open.

◆ Module 2　Learn to Read ◆

Warm-up

(1) Open.

(2) 1) 香山饭店 (the Fragrant Hill Hotel near Beijing)

2) 卢浮宫院内的玻璃金字塔 (a glass and steel pyramid for the Louvre Museum in Paris)

3) 肯尼迪图书馆 (the John Fitzgerald Kennedy Library near Boston)

4) 华盛顿国家艺术馆东馆 (the East Building of the National Gallery of Art, Washington, D. C.)

5) 苏州博物馆 (the Suzhou Museum in Jiangsu Province)

6) 香港中银大厦 (the Bank of China in Hong Kong)

(3) Open.

Passage A　Ieoh Ming Pei and the Louvre Pyramid
Reading Comprehension

1. *Global understanding*

(1) open.

(2) Ieoh Ming Pei placed a full-sized model of the pyramid in the courtyard of the Louvre.

(3) open.

2. *Detailed understanding*

(1) C　(2) B　(3) A　(4) B　(5) D

Language Practice

1. *Make sure you know the words in the table below. Choose the word or phrase to complete each of the following sentences. Change the form where necessary.*

(1) project　(2) eased　(3) estimated　(4) soothed

(5) a variety of　(6) agreed to　(7) serves as　(8) In an attempt to

2. *Complete the following sentences by translating into English the Chinese given in brackets.*

(1) he also took on some odd jobs

(2) When he grew up

(3) That expert laid out a project

(4) out of place with the occasion

70

(5) he was asked to serve as a secretary

3. *Translate the following sentences into Chinese, paying special attention to the coloured parts.*

(1) 去年,他去北京拜访了朋友。

(2) 迈克尔足球踢得好,上个月他被邀请进了校队。

(3) 为了通过考试,上个月他学习非常刻苦。

(4) 那人对公众的批评反应激烈。

(5) 上周我们的展览向公众开放了。

Passage B   Louis Vuitton

Reading Comprehension

1. *Global understanding*

(1) b   (2) c   (3) a

2. *Detailed understanding*

(1) D   (2) A   (3) D   (4) C   (5) B

Language Practice

1. *Match the words in Column A with the appropriate meanings in Clolumn B.*

(1) b   (2) e   (3) a   (4) d   (5) c

2. Open.

◆ Module 3   Culture Link ◆

1. Open.

2. *Work in groups to classify the following superstitions into two categories by filling in the boxes below.*

Category A: Good Luck

☐ To carry a rabbit's foot in your pocket.

☐ To bring a stick of coal to a friend's home, on New Year's Day.

☐ To put a penny in your shoe.

☐ To carry a piece of jade or tiger's eye.

Category B: Bad Luck

☐ To walk under a ladder.

☐ To have a black cat cross your path.

☐ To open an umbrella inside the home.

☐ To put your shoes on the bed/table/bench.

3. *Some people believe that some goods cannot be sent as gifts. Match the goods listed in Column A with their proper meanings listed in Column B.*

Goods that cannot be sent as gifts

☐ Knives—Cut the relationship with your friends.

☐ Bags—Encourage them to pack and leave the relationship.

☐ Shoes—Encourage them to walk out of the relationship.

☐ Perfumes—Attract a third party that can break up the relationship.

◆ Module 4　Scenario Link ◆

Open.

■ Tapescripts ■

◆ Lead-in ◆

The Suzhou Museum is situated in Suzhou, Jiangsu province. The current building was designed by Chinese-American architect Ieoh Ming Pei. Construction of this building started in 2002. It was inaugurated on October 6, 2006.

The museum has a display area of 2,200 square meters. It has more than 15,000 pieces in its collections. Most are ancient paintings and calligraphy, ceramics, crafts, unearthed relics and revolution relics. Among them 247 pieces are ranked first-class. It also has more than 70,000 books and documents, and over 20,000 rubbings of stone inscriptions. The collection of paintings and calligraphy includes works of masters from Song Dynasty to Ming and Qing Dynasties.

◆ Module 1　Learn to Talk ◆

Giving Opinions

3. *Listen to a conversation and fill in the blanks with the information you hear.*

John: Dad, what do you think of the famous architect Ieoh Ming Pei?

Father: Well, in my opinion, he is the only world-class Chinese architect of the 20th century.

John: I quite agree with you. He is truly an outstanding architect in the world.

Father: He grew up mostly in Hong Kong and Shanghai.

John: You're right. I feel his life in China had some influence on his work.

Father: Exactly. He said it did have an influence on his work. How do you feel about the Hong Kong Bank of China?

John: The architecture is beautiful.

Father: But some people may not think so. They are not pleased about it. They see the building as a sharp knife shining coldly in the center of Hong Kong.

Father: I think it's the influence of Chinese culture on people's view of things.

4. *Listen to and practise reading the following dialogue, paying attention to the coloured expressions and patterns.*

A: What do you think of the miniskirt at the fashion show last night?

B: Well, I think it's pretty short. It's not suitable for a Chinese girl to wear a skirt like that.

A: That's exactly what I think. It's only suitable for a supermodel on the catwalk.

B: Do you think people can wear that skirt and walk around the streets?

A: I'm not sure. Maybe some people certainly can. Don't forget it is already the 21st century.

B: Well, my mom would never let me wear a skirt like that.

A: I believe my mom wouldn't, either.

Stories of Designers and Their Works

1. *Listen to a short passage about the problem of Fengshui in architecture and decide whether the following statements are true (T) or false (F).*

Fengshui is the problem architects often meet. The most famous case of it in recent years was the building, the Hong Kong Bank of China. It was designed by Chinese-American architect Ieoh Ming Pei. After reviewing Pei's original blueprint of the building, the Bank of China sent a telegraph to him, expressing their concerns about the huge steel frames, which looked like squares with the letters Xs in them. Their worries came from China's belief that X means bad luck.

Finally Pei hid all these steel frames of the building and changed the Xs into lucky Buddhist symbols. This greatly pleased the bank.

Some fengshui experts still see the building as a sharp knife shinning coldly in the center of Hong Kong, while Pei designed it to look like a spring bamboo shoot suggesting the life of the bank.

From the scientific point of view, the X frames are reasonable and even beautiful in design; however, they look evil and ugly in Chinese people's eyes because they don't fit with Chinese culture. In this sense, fengshui can be considered the balance between science and culture.

2. *Listen to an interview with the car designer Ian Callum and fill in the blanks with the information you hear.*

In an interview, Ian Callum said when he was a kid, he used to write to dealers in Glasgow and Edinburgh, or even London, pretending he was a potential customer to get brochures. He also wrote to people to get information on how to become a car designer, but Jaguar was the only company he wrote to. He got a reply, too, telling him to study technical drawing.

When he was asked if it was American cars that had the greatest influence on his growing up, he gave a definite answer. He said American cars were the most expressive.

In an interview, he mentioned that as a junior designer for Ford, he felt really low for the first few months.

Text Translations

◆ Passage A ◆

贝聿铭与卢浮宫金字塔

贝聿铭是著名的现代建筑设计大师,美籍华裔,生于1917年,主要是在中国香港和上海长大。

1981年,当时新当选的法国总统提出了一些建筑项目,其中一项就是整修卢浮宫博物馆。贝聿铭应邀参与这项工程,在悄悄去法国考察三次之后,他最后答应接受这一工作。

贝聿铭的其中一项设计方案是在卢浮宫建一个玻璃和钢架的金字塔。这个玻璃金字塔用做卢浮宫博物馆的入口。但是,那个时候公众强力反对他的这个设计。因为,许多人认为这个玻璃和钢结构的金字塔与具有传统设计风格的卢浮宫博物馆看起来格格不入。

为了平息公众的不满,贝聿铭采纳了当时法国总统的建议,在卢浮宫院子里摆放了一个实际大小的金字塔。在接下来的4天时间里,大约有6万人前来参观,之后批评者们的反对意见消失了。

1989年3月,卢浮宫金字塔正式向公众开放。人们认为,它的建筑风格是旧与新、古典与现代的完美结合。现在,卢浮宫金字塔已成为巴黎城市的象征。

◆ Passage B ◆

路易威登

路易·威登(1821—1892)是路易威登毛利特公司的创始人。人们通常称该公司为路易威登公司,简称LV。这家公司是最著名的国际时装公司之一。路易·威登生于法国,1835年他徒步从家乡走到巴黎,在长达400公里的旅途中,他干过各种各样的零活,以贴补旅途之需。在巴黎,他做过专门给法国贵族制作箱包的学徒工。在这个行当他有良好声誉,拿破仑三世指名他作为自己的箱包制作人。这些经历使他积累了先进的箱包制作知识。此时,他开始了自己的箱包设计,这为LV公司的建立打下了基础。路易·威登去世后,他的儿子乔治·威登开始着手把公司做成一家全球性的公司。

路易威登通过分布在世界各地的自己的商店来销售产品。这种销售策略不仅使公司能够掌控商品的质量和价格,同时也很好地避免了一些假冒产品进入商品配送渠道。路易威登产品不打折,公司也不开免税商店,产品的配送完全由该公司自己完成。

路易威登是世界最知名的品牌之一,长久以来它是身份和财富的象征,公司的有些产品在国际时尚市场上价格是最高的。

Unit 6   Famous Singers

I. Background Information

In music, a song is a composition for voice or voices, performed by singing. A song may be accompanied by musical instruments, or it may be unaccompanied, as in the case of a cappella songs. The lyrics (words) of songs are typically of a poetic, rhyming nature, though they may be religious verses or free prose.

A song may be for a solo singer, a duet, trio, or larger ensemble involving more voices. Songs with more than one voice to a part are considered choral works. Songs can be broadly divided into many different forms, depending on the criteria used. One division is between "art songs", "pop songs", and "folk songs". Other common methods of classification are by purpose (sacred vs secular), by style (dance, ballad, lied, etc.), or by time of origin (Renaissance, Contemporary, etc.).

1. Art songs are songs created for performance in their own right, usually with piano accompaniment, although they can also have other types of accompaniment such as an orchestra or string quartet, and are always notated. Generally they have an identified author(s) and composer and require voice training for acceptable performances.

2. Folk songs are songs of often anonymous origin (or are public domain) that are transmitted orally. They are frequently a major aspect of national or cultural identity. Art songs often approach the status of folk songs when people forget who the author was. Folk songs are also frequently transmitted non-orally (that is, as sheet music), especially in the modern era. Folk songs exist in almost every, if not all, culture(s).

3. Modern popular songs are typically distributed as recordings, and are played on the radio, though all other mass media that have audio capabilities are involved. Their relative popularity is inferred from commercially significant sales of recordings, ratings of stations and networks that play them, and ticket sales for concerts by the recording artists. A popular song can become a modern folk song when members of the public who learn to sing it from the recorded version teach their version to others. Popular songs may be called pop songs for short, although pop songs or pop music may instead be considered a more commercially popular genre of popular music as a whole.

Singers are often accompanied by musicians and instruments, while other people sing to have fun. Vocal skill is usually a combination of innate talent and professional training. Professional singers usually undergo voice training, provided by a voice teacher or coach.

◆ **Human voice**

In European classical music and opera, voices are treated as musical instruments. Composers who write vocal music must have an understanding of the skills, talents, and vocal properties of

75

singers.

Singers usually build their careers around certain musical styles. Voice classification systems have evolved to classify singers by tessitura(声域), vocal weight and timbre(音色). Choral singers are classified by vocal range. Other categories are soubrette, heldentenor, coloratura, and basso buffo.

There are also categories for men who are capable of singing in the female range. This type of voice is very rare, but it is still being used in opera.

Singers are also classified by the style of music they sing, such as soul singers or carnatic vocalists.

◆**Lead and backing vocalists**

In many modern musical groups, there is one singer that is singing the main parts (the lead vocalist) and one or more to perform backing vocals. Backing vocalists sing some, but usually not all, parts of the song. They often provide a harmony to the lead, or just sing along in the refrain or hum in the background. An exception is five-part gospel, a cappella music, where the lead is the highest of the five voices and sings a descant, and not the melody.

II. Notes

1. Notes to Lead-in

(1) Elvis Aaron Presley

埃尔维斯·亚伦·普雷斯利(1935—1977),"猫王"是他的昵称。他与鲍勃·迪伦、披头士并称摇滚乐史上最伟大的不朽象征。他的音乐超越了种族以及文化的疆界,将乡村音乐、布鲁斯音乐以及山地摇滚乐融会贯通,形成了具有鲜明个性的独特曲风,强烈地震撼了当时的流行乐坛。

(2) *Love Me Tender*

歌名《温柔地爱我》,电影译名《铁血柔情》。1956 年秋,猫王以处女作《温柔地爱我》闯入电影界。他在电影里无论饰演什么角色,只要有他演唱的歌曲,这部电影就会成为世界畅销影片。作为猫王出演的第一部电影,曾被批评为 B 级闹剧,是一部相当俗套的爱情故事,但这部电影的票房却很成功。片中的金曲 *Love Me Tender* 后来也占据了全美四项排行冠军。不久,包括衬衫、围巾、牛仔裤和口红在内的二十多种"猫王"品牌商品接连问世。

2. Notes to Module 1

(1) Luciano Pavarotti

鲁契亚诺·帕瓦罗蒂(1935—2007),世界著名的意大利男高音歌唱家。帕瓦罗蒂早年是小学教师,1961 年在阿基莱·佩里国际声乐比赛中,因成功演唱歌剧《波希米亚人》主角鲁道夫的咏叹调,荣获一等奖,从此开始歌唱生涯。1964 年首次在米兰·斯卡拉歌剧院登台,次年应邀去澳大利亚演出及录制唱片。1967 年被卡拉扬挑选为威尔第《安魂曲》的男高音独唱者。从此,声名节节上升,成为活跃于国际歌剧舞台上的最佳男高音之一。帕瓦罗蒂具有十分漂亮的音色,在两个八度以上的整个音域里,所有音均能迸射出明亮、晶莹的光辉。其著名的歌剧角色包括《里戈莱托》中的曼亚诺公爵和《爱达》中的拉达梅斯。

（2）Modena

摩德纳，意大利北部城市，位于波河的南岸，艾米利亚—罗马涅大区摩德纳省省会。摩德纳是意大利传统的工业、农业重镇，也是意大利最安全的风景游览胜地和最重要的历史文化名城之一，它拥有意大利"美食天堂"的美誉。摩德纳市也被称为"世界名车之都"、"引擎之都"，因为"玛莎拉迪"、"法拉利"、"布佳迪"、"兰博基尼"等多家世界顶级汽车公司总部都设在摩德纳市的郊区。

（3）Jose Carreras

何塞·卡雷拉斯，西班牙男高音，1946 年 12 月 5 日出生于加泰隆尼亚自治区首府巴塞罗那。求学和第一次登台演出都是在家乡，演出的剧目是威尔第《那布果》。1971 年卡雷拉斯获得意大利"威尔第声乐大奖"，逐渐成为世界顶级的抒情男高音。卡雷拉斯和帕瓦罗蒂、多明戈是享誉世界的三大男高音。

（4）Placido Domingo

普拉希多·多明戈，西班牙歌剧歌唱家，生于 1941 年，因其抒情、戏剧性的出色表演而著名。多明戈出生于马德里，父母均是西班牙民族歌剧演员，9 岁时全家迁居墨西哥。青年时期多明戈热衷于斗牛和唱歌，于席德音乐学院毕业后入墨西哥国家歌剧院唱男中音。20 岁那年，多明戈以演唱《茶花女》中的阿尔弗莱德跨入男高音的行列，同年与著名女高音歌唱家萨瑟兰在美国同台演出歌剧《拉美莫尔的露契亚》，1965 年起在马赛、维也纳、汉堡、柏林、纽约、伦敦等著名歌剧院演出。他的演唱嗓音丰满华丽，坚强有力，胜任从抒情到戏剧型的各类男高音角色。他塑造的奥赛罗、拉达美斯等形象，富于强烈的戏剧性和悲剧色彩。他还演唱过不少脍炙人口的小曲，又是位颇得好评的钢琴家和指挥家。其中，1992 年巴塞罗那奥运会开幕式上的会歌就是由他和一位女高音歌唱家演唱的。

（5）Anna Moffo

安娜·莫福（1932—2006），意大利女高音歌唱家，出生于美国宾夕法尼亚州一个有意大利血统的鞋匠家庭。1954 年，她加入了费城爱乐乐团并通过"年轻艺术家声乐考试"，在费城科蒂斯音乐学院从格莱戈里主修声乐。她获得了"富布莱特法案基金会"奖学金，去到罗马深入学习声乐、意大利语和歌剧演出。因在意大利斯波莱托剧院和电视节目中演出《蝴蝶夫人》获得成功而相继登上皮亚琴察和斯卡拉歌剧院的舞台，并去萨尔兹堡、伦敦、巴黎等地巡回演出。1957 年在美国芝加哥抒情歌剧院以《艺术家的生涯》中的咪咪一角引起轰动。两年后又在纽约大都会歌剧院成功地演唱了《蝴蝶夫人》《茶花女》等剧目，为国际歌剧所赞赏。她音质纯净清脆，线条明晰匀称，音量不大，却充盈着极强的艺术感染力。

（6）Pennsylvania

宾夕法尼亚州，位于美国东部，为立国 13 州之一。1787 年 12 月 12 日，联邦宪法批准宾夕法尼亚成为加入联邦的第二个州。宾夕法尼亚州在美国独立战争及新共和国成立中起重要作用，首府为哈里斯堡，最大城市是费城。

（7）James Levine

詹姆斯·莱文（1943—　），美国指挥家。幼年是钢琴神童，后进朱里亚德音乐学院，学习钢琴与指挥。1964 年任克利夫兰交响乐团指挥大师赛尔身边的副指挥，1970 年在美国许多乐团任客座指挥，1971 年在大都会歌剧院因指挥普契尼的《托斯卡》获巨大成功而被聘为首席，1975 年又被授予音乐指导。1976 年，年仅

33 岁的莱文就任大都会歌剧院音乐总监,成为该院任期最久的音乐总监之一。1986 年,升为该院艺术总监,这是大都会歌剧院一百多年来的历史性突破。目前,大都会歌剧院在莱文的领导下演出水准不断提高,有直追米兰斯卡拉歌剧院之势。大都会歌剧院是他的大本营,另外,他还经常赴欧洲任客席指挥。自1975 年起,他曾先后 6 次在萨尔茨堡音乐节中指挥演出,剧目是莫扎特的《蒂托的仁慈》《魔笛》《伊多梅纽》《费加罗的婚礼》、奥芬巴赫的《夫曼的故事》、勋伯格《摩西与亚伦》等。1982 年,莱文在拜罗伊特音乐节上首次指挥演出瓦格纳首演100 周年纪念的歌剧《帕西法尔》。在欧洲,他还经常联同柏林爱乐乐团、维也纳爱乐乐团等举行音乐会。

(8)Philadelphia

　　费城,美国宾夕法尼亚州最大的城市,位于该州东南部、特拉华河与斯库尔基尔河的交汇处。它由威廉·彭于 1681 年在原瑞典领地上建立起来。1774 年和 1775 年两次大陆会议在这里召开;1776 年 7 月 4 日《独立宣言》在这里签署;1787 年制宪会议在该城市召开;从 1790 年到 1800 年曾作为美国的首都。因此,费城被称为美利坚合众国的摇篮。

(9)Curtis Institute of Music

　　柯蒂斯音乐学院,位于美国费城,由玛丽·路易斯·科蒂斯·博克创建于 1924 年 10 月,是世界上最有名的音乐学院之一。学院从创办之日起就在作曲、指挥、声乐、管弦乐、键盘乐等领域提供最优秀的教学,学院也因此获得"独奏家摇篮"的美誉。柯蒂斯音乐学院是由宾夕法尼亚州联邦特许,宾州高等院校学位教育委员会注册的音乐学院,是美国国家音乐院校联合会的主要成员。1993 年获得美国中部各州高校联合会高等教育委员会的认可。柯蒂斯音乐学院对所有学生都提供全额奖学金,但是学院的录取也非常严格,每年平均只招收 160 名新生。学校的办学理念是"为那些最具音乐天赋的年轻人提供最优质的教育,并将他们培养成最专业的艺术家"。学院每年为学生提供大量公开演出的机会,这一方式使得学校在近百年的历史中,培养了许许多多著名的艺术家。

(10)Fulbright Award

　　富布赖特奖学金。"富布赖特科学奖学金计划"是美国与其他约 150 个国家和地区之间签订的学术交流计划。能够入选"富布赖特科学奖学金计划"的学生,要由一流专家小组推选并在全球竞争产生,而不是通过传统的双边协议来推出。对这些研究生的资助时间也要长于传统的 3 年期。发起者富布赖特(1905—1995),美国政治人物。在阿肯色大学毕业后,去英国牛津大学深造,回国后在阿肯色大学任教,1939—1941 年任该校校长。1942 年富布赖特当选众议员,在参议院(1945—1975)任职期间,他提出的建立国际交流计划"富布赖特奖学金"被通过。

3. Notes to Module 2

(1)Paul Robeson

　　保罗·罗伯逊(1898—1976),美国著名男低音歌唱家、演员、社会活动家。早年在穆维尔高级学校求学期间,他就曾参加过莎士比亚戏剧的演出。1923 年罗伯逊毕业于哥伦比亚大学法律系,此后一直从事戏剧演出和电影拍摄等活动。1925 年罗伯逊在纽约哈伦剧院举行第一次黑人灵歌独唱会,大获成功。1927 年,他在美国著名音乐剧《游览船》中演唱了《老人河》一曲,由此一举成名。他通晓多种语言,能用英、法、俄、汉等二十余种语言歌唱,其音色浑厚、深沉,具有黑人歌唱家所特有的魅力。

(2) Assembly of God Church

神召会教堂。神召会(Assemblies of God)是 1901 年美国五旬节复兴运动后出现的教会组织。三百多位传道人和信徒于 1914 年在美国阿肯色州热泉城召开大会成立,成为 20 世纪早期从"五旬节派"运动中产生出来的最大的一个教派。1924 年,于英国成立该派教会并成立神召会国际联合组织。1960 年代中期,有 8 500 座教会,登记的教徒约 55.6 万人,有约 9 000 所主日学校(Sunday School),学员总数约 100 万人。

(3) Gospel music

福音音乐。福音音乐是历史上美国的黑人农奴接受了基督教的信仰之后,常在田里祈祷,希望减少劳动的痛苦,不久便演变成即兴的音乐表演。在奴隶制废除之后,黑人们组织了自己的教堂,并把这种音乐形式作为教堂活动的一种。福音音乐主要强调有节奏的器乐伴奏和即兴演唱。20 世纪中期,猫王把福音音乐引进到自己的音乐风格中。

(4) Princeton

普林斯顿,美国新泽西州中部城市,享有自治权。1696 年由贵格教派建立,是普林斯顿大学所在地。

(5) New Jersey

新泽西州,位于美国大西洋沿岸。17 世纪 20 年代和 30 年代被荷兰和瑞典殖民者占领,1664 年作为新荷兰的一部分割让给英国,1702 年成为一个皇家省。这块殖民地在美国独立战争中具有重大战略意义,是几大战役的战场。

(6) Protestant

新教是与东正教、天主教并列的三大基督教派别之一,为 16 世纪宗教改革运动中脱离天主教而形成的各个新宗教,以及从这些宗派中不断分化出来的各个新宗派的统称。中国的新教各教会则自称基督教或耶稣教,而不称新教。

(7) Yiddish

依地语。历史上中欧和东欧的犹太人所用的国际语,是多种语言的混合,主要来自于中世纪日耳曼方言,其次来自于希伯来语、阿拉姆语和各种斯拉夫语、古法语及古意大利语。

(8) African American spiritual music

非裔美国黑人所创的圣歌,是北美黑人的宗教礼拜歌曲。内容大多反映黑人遭受残酷奴役,痛苦无告,只好把希望寄托在宗教上的悲惨处境。歌曲用英语演唱,其旋律朴素,富于节奏感,和声近似美国基督教会的赞美诗。由于经常即兴演唱,几乎没有定谱可以遵循。南北战争后,由于菲斯克大学黑人歌唱团等黑人歌手的传布,以美国最有代表性的黑人民歌闻名于世,并成为爵士音乐的重要素材。

4. Notes to Module 3

Traditional and Modern Chinese Festivals

Chinese people celebrate a series of festivals during the course of a year. Most of these festivals take place on important dates in the Chinese lunar calendar. The following are important traditional and modern festivals celebrated by Chinese people.

Spring Festival

Spring Festival (Lunar New Year's Day) falls on the 1st day of the 1st lunar month, often one month later than the Gregorian calendar. People attach great importance to Spring Festival Eve. At that time, all family members eat dinner together which is called Reunion Dinner. The meal is more luxurious than usual. Dishes such as chicken, fish and bean curd cannot be excluded, for in Chinese, their pronunciations, respectively "ji", "yu" and "doufu", mean auspiciousness, abundance and richness. After the dinner, the whole family will sit together, chatting and watching TV. According to custom, each family will stay up to see the New Year in.

Mid-Autumn Festival

The Mid-Autumn Festival falls on the 15th day of the 8th lunar month, usually in October in Solar calendar. People will enjoy the full moon and eat moon cakes on that day. On the Mid-Autumn Festival, family members or friends meet outside, putting food on tables and looking up into the sky while talking about life. How splendid a moment it is!

National Day

October 1st is the commemoration day of the founding of New China; it is also Chinese National Day. On 1st October, 1949, Chairman Mao Zedong in Tiananmen Square raised the first five-star red flag (the national flag of the People's Republic of China) and solemnly declared to the world that the People's Republic of China was then established.

Lantern Festival

Lantern Festival falls on the 15th of the first lunar month. There is the custom of enjoying lantern shows and eating sweet dumplings. There are also activities like walking on stilts and answering riddles written on lanterns.

Tomb-sweeping Day

Tomb-sweeping Day (Qing Ming Festival) is a time to remember the dead and pay respect to one's deceased (已故的) ancestors and family members. Because it reinforces the ethic of filial piety, Qing Ming is a major Chinese festival. Literally meaning "clear" (Qing) and "bright" (Ming), this Chinese festival falls on the 4th, 5th or 6th day of April. It is an occasion for the whole family to sweep the graves of their forebears (祖先). Besides the tradition of honoring the dead, people also go outing, fly kites and launch a series of sports.

Dragon Boat Festival

The fifth of the fifth lunar month of the year is Dragon Boat Festival to commemorate the heroic suicide of Qu Yuan, an ancient Chinese poet who threw himself into a river when his earlier predictions of political disaster-ignored by the emperor-came true. The dragon boat race emulates the action of the inhabitants in Qu's hometown, who rowed their boats on the river on hearing of his tragic death. Now, it is celebrated as a custom by watching dragonboat races, and eating sticky rice wrapped in bamboo leaves.

Double Seventh Festival

Double Seventh Festival, on the 7th day of the 7th lunar month, is a traditional festival full of romance. At night when the sky is dotted with stars, people can see the Milky Way spanning from the north to the south. On each side of it is a bright star, which is imagined to be the Cowherd and Weaver Maid, and about them there is a beautiful love story passed down from generation to generation. Under the influence of Western countries, an increasing number of couples in China see that day as Chinese Valentine's Day.

Double Ninth Festival

The 9th day of the 9th lunar month is Double Ninth Festival, also known as Height Ascending Festival. It is also a time when chrysanthemum blooms. So climbing mountains, enjoying the flourishing chrysanthemum and drinking chrysanthemum wine and other outdoor activities have become popular on this day. In 1989, the Chinese government decided the day as Festival for the Elderly.

III. Language Points

Passage A

◆ Important Words ◆

raise['reɪz]*vt.* to care for a child or young animal until it is able to take care of himself/herself/itself 抚养；养育

e. g.　1. In those days, it took a whole village to raise a child.

　　　2. We have parents who raise us and love us.

attend[ə'tend]*vt.* to be present at an event 出席，参加（某场合）

e. g.　1. Most had confirmed that their head of state would attend the conference.

　　　2. It was a privilege for us to attend the ceremony.

influence['ɪnfluəns]*n.* the effect that sb/sth has on the way a person thinks or behaves or on the way that sth works or develops 影响；改变

e. g.　1. My teacher's influence made me study science at college.

　　　2. Her parents considered her friend to be a bad influence on her.

pursue[pə'sjuː]*vt.* to do sth or try to achieve sth over a period of time 追求；致力于

e. g.　1. She wished to pursue a medical career.

　　　2. Turn away from evil and do good, seek peace and pursue it.

be devoted to 深爱着；致力于

e. g.　1. She is devoted to her studies.

2. He is devoted to helping those who suffer.

have faith in 相信；信仰

e. g.   1. We know we should have faith in ourselves.

2. I have much faith in your ability to win the game.

other than 除了……以外；不包括

e. g.   1. There's nobody here other than me.

2. You can't get there other than by swimming.

◆Explanation of Difficult Sentences◆

(1) Presley got his first guitar at the age of ten, and had his first taste of musical success when he won a talent show at Humes High School in Memphis.

- 普雷斯利 10 岁那年,因为在孟菲斯休姆中学举办的业余歌手演唱会上获奖,得到了平生第一把吉他,首次体尝到音乐成功的喜悦。

- talent show 意为业余歌手演唱会,目前很多场合音译成"达人秀"。

(2) Presley began touring and recording, trying to get his first big break.

- 普雷斯利开始巡回演出并录制唱片,力求撞上人生第一次大运。

- 句中有三个动词-ing 形式,但在句中功能不尽相同。主句后跟上"trying to…"这一分词短语,补充说明猫王巡游演出和录制唱片的目的。而 begin 后跟的是宾语 touring and recording。

   另外,begin 可以跟 to 不定式或 v-ing 动名词形式,但如果 begin 后接的是表示心里活动的动词,如 think, realize, understand 等,或 begin 本身为-ing 形式时,其后通常要接不定式而不接动名词。如:She began to understand.

(3) Music industry experts say more than one thousand million of Elvis's recordings have sold throughout the world.

- 唱片业的专家称,普雷斯利的唱片在全世界的销量超过了 10 亿张。

- 句中在 one thousand million 属于英式表达,在美式英语中,用 billion 表示 thousand million。
   句中 sell 习惯用作主动语态,但实际表达被动意义,如:

This book sells well.

The house is to sell.

(4) He was a success in many different kinds of music—popular, country, religious, and rhythm and blues.

- 他在流行音乐、乡村音乐、宗教音乐以及节奏布鲁斯音乐等多种音乐门类中都很成功。

- success 在句中意为 a successful person,指成功的人(或物)。rhythm 指节奏音乐,blues 指布鲁斯歌

曲,也称蓝调音乐。rhythm and blues 是将前两者的风格有机结合而形成的新型音乐,即"节奏蓝调"。

Passage B

◆ Important Words ◆

former[ˈfɔːmə(r)] a. that used to exist in earlier times 从前的,以前的;denoting the first or first mentioned of two people or things 前一个的

e. g.　1. The owner of the shop is Mr Brown, the former owner being Mr Johnson.

　　　2. Between swimming and football, he preferred the former.

part[ˈpɑːt] n. a role played by an actor in a play, film/movie, etc. ; the words spoken by an actor in a particular role(剧中的)角色;台词

e. g.　Which part do you play?

　　　1. Have you learnt your part by heart?

　　　2. The part of Hamlet was played by Laurence Olivier.

criticize[ˈkrɪtɪsaɪz] vt. to say that you disapprove of sb/sth; to say what you do not like or think is wrong about sb/sth 批评;责备

e. g.　1. Would you like to read and criticize my new book?

　　　2. People often criticize TV for showing too much sex and violence.

instead[ɪnˈsted] ad. in the place of sb/sth 代替;顶替

e. g.　1. I didn't have a pen, so I used a pencil instead.

　　　2. If you cannot go, he'll go instead of you.

seek[siːk] vt. to look for sb/sth; to try to obtain or achieve sth 寻找;寻求

e. g.　1. We are born to seek truth.

　　　2. China's booming economy is attracting many foreigners to seek work here.

fluent[ˈfluːənt] a. (of a person) able to express oneself easily and accurately 流利的;流畅的

e. g.　1. He is fluent in a dozen foreign languages.

　　　2. She gave a fluent performance of the sonata.

include[ɪnˈkluːd] vt. to take in as a part, an element, or a member; to contain as a secondary or subordinate element 包括;包含

e. g.　1. The university includes ten colleges.

　　　2. The list included his name.

diverse[daɪˈvɜːs]*a.* very different from each other and of various kinds 各种各样的；不同的；变化多的

e. g.　1. In a country as diverse as South Africa, all this is to be expected.

　　　　2. My friend and I have diverse ideas on how to raise children.

become involved in 参与；卷入

e. g.　1. One day, the farmer became involved in a dispute with his neighbor over a cow.

　　　　2. After retirement, she became involved in voluntary services in the local community.

◆Explanation of Difficult Sentences◆

（1）Paul was an excellent student and athlete.

● 保罗既是一名优秀的学生，也是一名优秀的运动员。

● 句中主语补足成份 student and athlete 同指 Paul，故只用一个冠词，不能说成 Paul was an excellent student and an athlete.

（2）He criticized the American movie industry for not showing the real lives of black people in America.

● 他批评美国电影业没有反映美国黑人的真实生活。

● criticize 通常作及物动词，意为"批评，责备"，后面接介宾短语"for…"解释批评或责备的原因。非谓语动词，如动名词 *v*-ing 可以和介词 for 配合使用，在句中常表示目的、原因等。

show the real life of sb 可直接理解为"展示……的真实生活"。

（3）He stopped making movies and decided to sing professionally instead.

● 他不再演电影，转而决定从事专业演唱。

● stop 后面可接宾语，如 stop doing sth，表示"停止做某事"；后面也可以接目的状语，如 stop to do sth, 表示"（把原先在做的事情）停下来而换做某事"。

IV. Keys, Tapescripts and Text Translations

■■ Keys ■■

◆Lead-in◆

1. *Here is a song by Elvis Presley. Listen carefully and take down the missing words.*

Love Me Tender

Love me tender, 温柔地爱我，

Love me sweet, 甜蜜地爱我，

Never let me go. 不要让我离开。

You have made my life complete, 你让我的生活变得完美，

And I love you so. 我是多么地爱你。

Love me tender, 温柔地爱我,

Love me true, 真挚地爱我,

All my dreams fulfilled. 我所有愿望都实现了。

For my darling I love you, 因为亲爱的我爱你,

And I always will. 我会一直爱着你。

Love me tender, 温柔地爱我,

Love me long, 长久地爱我,

Take me to your heart. 让我进入你的内心。

For it's there that I belong, 因为我属于那里,

And we'll never part. 我们永远不会分开。

Love me tender, 温柔地爱我,

Love me true, 真挚地爱我,

All my dreams fulfilled. 我所有愿望都实现了。

For my darlin' I love you, 因为亲爱的我爱你,

And I always will. 我会一直爱着你。

Love me tender, 温柔地爱我,

Love me dear, 深情地爱我,

Tell me you are mine. 告诉我你是我的。

I'll be yours through all the years, 穿越岁月,我将永远属于你,

Till the end of time. 直至天荒地老。

Love me tender, 温柔地爱我,

Love me true, 真挚地爱我,

All my dreams fulfilled. 我所有愿望都实现了。

For my darlin' I love you, 因为亲爱的我爱你,

And I always will. 我会一直爱着你。

2. Open.

◆Module 1   Learn to Talk◆

Expressing Willingness & Wishes

1. *David and Nancy meet each other on campus. Listen to the model dialogue, and underline the expressions of willingness and wishes.*

David: How have you been recently?

Nancy: Not too bad. How about you?

David: Same as ever. But I'm looking forward to a relaxing weekend.

Nancy: I hope I can find free time too. I've been a little busy this week.

David: How do you want to spend this weekend?

Nancy: I wish to see some movies or read something.

David: Oh? I have got two tickets for tomorrow's solo concert. Will you join me?

Nancy: Really? I'm glad to. Thanks.

David: By the way, why not take a digital camera with you?

Nancy: Good idea! I'd rather it didn't rain tomorrow.

David: I heard the weather should be good except for some shower in the morning.

Nancy: That's good. Then we'll have a good weekend.

David: Sure. I'll be waiting for you at the front gate around 2:30 P.M.

Nancy: OK. See you then.

2. Open.

3. *Listen to the dialogue between John and Lucy. Decide whether the following statements are true (T) or false (F).*

    (1)F (2)T (3)F (4)F (5)T (6)F

4. Open. 5. Open. 6. Open.

Stories of Famous Singers

Before You Listen

1. Open. 2. Open.

While You Listen

1. *Listen and answer the questions about the two singers Luciano Pavarotti and Anna Moffo. Check (√) the correct box.*

Who...	Luciano Pavarotti	Anna Moffo
1. was born in the U.S.?	☐	√
2. was born in Italy?	√	☐
3. began performing at age nine?	√	☐
4. studied at the Curtis Institute of Music?	☐	√
5. sang with famous pop, rock and jazz singers?	√	☐
6. was offered work in Hollywood movies after graduating from high school?	☐	√
7. won a Fulbright Award to study in Italy?	☐	√
8. was one of the "Three Tenors"?	√	☐

2. *Listen again and fill in the following table about Luciano Pavarotti and Anna Moffo.*

	Evaluations
Luciano Pavarotti	(1) Some people criticized Luciano Pavarotti <u>for extending his music beyond the limits of opera</u>. (2) But many <u>opera lovers and experts</u> were thankful for his common touch. (3) James Levine of the Metropolitan Opera House in New York City said Pavarotti's singing "spoke right to <u>the hearts of listeners</u>, whether they knew anything about opera or not".
Anna Moffo	(1) Anna Moffo's star <u>in the opera world</u> burned brightly but also briefly. (2) She said she worked too hard and travelled too much <u>early in her career</u>. (3) Her career was <u>mostly over</u> by the 1970s.

After You Listen

Open.

◆Module 2 Learn to Read◆

Warm-up

Open.

Passage A Life of Elvis Presley

Reading Comprehension

1. *Global understanding*

   (1) The passage mainly relates some musical influences upon Elvis Presley in his early life and how he pursued his musical dream.

   (2) Open.

   (3) Open.

2. *Detailed understanding*

   (1) C   (2) B   (3) D   (4) B   (5) C

Language Practice

1. Open.

2. *Identify the musical terms or expressions in the passage. Then think of a word or expression which is similar to each of them.*

Musical terms or expressions	Similar words or expressions
gospel music	religious music / spiritual music / church music
recording	demo record / album / single
talent show	amateur performance / musical contest
country music	pop song / folk song / ballad
rhythm and blues	rock music / waltz / tango

3. *Translate the following sentences, paying special attention to the coloured parts.*

   (1) a. 他深爱自己的父母,尤其是母亲。

   b. 这位护士兢兢业业地看护着病人。

   (2) a. 这位歌手将自己的巡回演出情况做了记载。

   b. 唱片版权商萨姆·菲利普斯决定将这位年轻的歌手纳入自己的保护之下。

   (3) a. 猫王是在充满爱的工薪族父母的呵护和抚养下成长起来的,一家人由于生活拮据,四处迁徙。

   b. 他不得不提高嗓门,好让听众都听得见。

   (4) 普雷斯利曾经跟父母一起去神召会教堂,那里的福音音乐对他产生了深远影响。

   (5) 普雷斯利10岁那年,在孟菲斯休姆中学举办的业余歌手演唱会上获了奖,得到了平生第一把吉他,并初次体尝到音乐成功的喜悦。

Passage B   American Singer Paul Robeson

Reading Comprehension

1. *Global understanding*

   Paragraph 1：b   Paragraph 2：d   Paragraph 3：a   Paragraph 4：c

2. *Detailed understanding*

   (1) B   (2) D   (3) A   (4) C

3. *Information scanning*

Time	What Paul Robeson experienced
In 1898	(1) He was born in Princeton, New Jersey.
(2) While at Rutgers	He played four sports.
In 1919	(3) He graduated from college.
(4) After the 1920s	His standard repertoire included songs in many languages.
(5) In the 1920's and 1930's	He appeared in eleven movies.
In the late 1930's	(6) He became involved in national and international movements.

Language Practice

1. *Make sure you know the words in the table below. Choose the word to complete each of the following sentences. Change the form where necessary.*

   (1) professional   (2) criticized   (3) instead   (4) diverse   (5) fluent

2. *Complete the following sentences by translating into English the Chinese given in brackets.*

   (1) It was not until the end of the performance that

   (2) to get involved in such kind of activity

   (3) showed the real lives of singers

   (4) is limited by its times

   (5) could express the same feelings

◆Module 3　Culture Link◆

Quiz

(1) Mid-Autumn Festival　　　(2) Chinese National Day
(3) Spring Festival　　　　　(4) Double Ninth Festival
(5) Lantern Festival　　　　　(6) Dragon Boat Festival
(7) Tomb-sweeping Day　　　 (8) Double Seventh Festival

◆Module 4　Scenario Link◆

Open.

■■■■ Tapescripts ■■■■

◆Module 1　Learn to Talk◆

Expressing Willingness & Wishes

3. *Listen to the dialogue between John and Lucy. Decide whether the following statements are true (T) or false (F).*

John: How time flies! How are things with you, Lucy?

Lucy: Pretty good, John. Have you finished your graduation paper?

John: Yes. What do you want to do when you graduate?

Lucy: I used to dream of becoming a professional singer, but now I want to work in a local TV station. What about you?

John: I'd rather take further courses for a Master's degree.

Lucy: That's good. In that case, you'll have a better chance to get a good job.

John: I suppose so, but competition is getting more intense every day.

Lucy: Why worry? As long as you plan carefully, most things are possible.

John: Yeah. I think it's important to be successful in a field you truly love, not something other people impose on you.

Lucy: You said it. My parents wanted me to work in a law firm, but I know that sort of job doesn't suit me.

John: I hope my parents won't try to interfere in my choice of career.

Stories of Singers

Luciano Pavarotti

Luciano Pavarotti was born near Modena in 1935. His father was a baker who loved to sing. As a child, Luciano listened to many great Italian opera singers in his father's record collection. He began performing when he was nine years old.

Pavarotti sang many other kinds of songs besides opera. He sang with famous pop, rock and jazz singers. He recorded Christmas songs, Italian folk songs and other kinds of music. Pavarotti also made popular recordings with two other famous opera singers, Jose Carreras and Placido Domingo. The group became known as the Three Tenors.

Some people criticized Luciano Pavarotti for extending his music beyond the limits of opera. But many opera lovers and experts were thankful for his common touch. James Levine of the Metropolitan Opera House in New York City said Pavarotti's singing "spoke right to the hearts of listeners, whether they knew anything about opera or not."

Anna Moffo

Anna Moffo was born in Wayne, Pennsylvania. Her beautiful soprano voice was discovered at a school music event when she was just seven years old.

Moffo was a very beautiful young woman. She was offered work in Hollywood movies right after she graduated from high school. But she wanted to sing. Moffo went to Philadelphia to study at the Curtis Institute of Music. Later she won a Fulbright Award to study in Italy. She performed in her first professional opera there in 1955. Two years later, Anna Moffo sang professionally for the first time in the United States.

Anna Moffo's star in the opera world burned brightly but also briefly. She said she worked too hard and traveled too much early in her career. It was mostly over by the 1970s.

■■■ Text Translation ■■■

◆ Passage A ◆

猫王生平

猫王普雷斯利一家生活拮据,四处迁徙。但他深爱自己的父母,特别是母亲格拉迪斯,而且由于从小受到(宗教)熏陶,对上帝十分虔诚。他曾随父母一起去神召会教堂,那里的福音音乐对他产生了深远影响。

普雷斯利10岁那年,因为在孟菲斯休姆中学举办的业余歌手演唱会上获奖,得到了平生第一把吉他,并初次体尝到音乐成功带来的喜悦。1953年高中毕业后,他在追寻音乐之梦的同时,还干过多种活儿。同年,他在一家后来被称为"阳光唱片公司"的录音棚里录制了第一盘试音带。不久,唱片版权商萨姆·菲利普斯决定将这位年轻的歌手纳入其翼下。歌曲《不错》(*That's All Right*)是猫王在1954年录制的第一支单曲。从此,他开始巡回演出,并录制唱片,力求撞上人生第一次大运。

不久,他靠一支歌曲打开了局面。《猎狗》(*Hound Dog*)是猫王普雷斯利最受欢迎的唱片之一。1956年,该唱片销量达500万张。唱片业的专家说,普雷斯利的唱片在全世界的销量超过10亿张。他在流行音乐、乡村音乐、宗教音乐以及节奏蓝调等多种音乐门类中都获得了成功。

猫王普雷斯利曾获得世界上许多国家的奖项,然而,除了英语之外,他没有录制过其他语言的唱片。除了在加拿大演出过三场,他再没有到美国以外的其他国家演出过。不过,他的唱片和电影至今仍受到世界各地人民的喜爱。

◆Passage B◆

美国歌唱家保罗·罗伯逊

1898 年，保罗·罗伯逊出生在新泽西州的普林斯顿。他的父亲以前曾是奴隶,后来成为新教教会的领导人。保罗是一位优秀的学生和运动员,新泽西的罗格斯大学给他提供奖学金,这样一来,他才得以进入大学学习,直到 1919 年毕业。在罗格斯大学求学期间,他参加了四项体育比赛,而且还是班上的尖子生。班上的同学们认为他将来会成为美国黑人的领袖。

在 20 世纪 20 年代和 30 年代,保罗·罗伯逊还出演过 11 部电影。不过,他发现自己的表演受到了限制,因为黑人所能扮演的角色有限。他批评美国电影业没有反映美国黑人的真实生活,并决定不再演电影,转而从事专业演唱。

罗伯逊演唱过多种门类的歌曲。他通过歌唱来支持当时的劳工运动和社会运动;他为和平和正义而唱。此外,他还演唱非裔美国人的宗教音乐。20 世纪 30 年代后期,保罗·罗伯逊开始关心国内和国际上寻求和平和改善劳工条件的运动。他支持非洲殖民地摆脱欧洲殖民统治、争取独立的斗争。

罗伯逊对世界各国的民族音乐也感兴趣。他渐渐地通晓了 20 种语言,能流利或基本流利地使用 12 种语言。在 20 世纪 20 年代之后他的常备节目中包括多种语言,有汉语、俄语、依地语以及德语等。他说,这些民歌和非裔美国人民的音乐一样,也表达了同样的情感。

Unit 7　Photographers

I. Background Information

A photographer is a person who takes photographs using a camera. A professional photographer uses photography to earn money whilst amateur photographers take photographs for pleasure and to record an event, emotion, a place, or a person.

A professional photographer may be an employee, for example, of a newspaper, or may contract to cover a particular event such as a wedding or graduation, or to illustrate an advertisement. Others, including paparazzi and fine art photographers, are freelancers, first making a picture and then offering it for sale or display. Some workers, such as policemen, estate agents, journalists and scientists, make photographs as part of other work. Photographers who produce moving rather than still pictures are often called cinematographers, videographers or camera operators, depending on the commercial context.

Photographers are also categorized based on the subjects they photograph. Some photographers explore subjects typical of paintings such as landscape, still life, and portraiture. Other photographers specialize in subjects unique to photography, including street photography, documentary photography, fashion photography, wedding photography, war photography, photojournalism, and commercial photography.

II. Notes

1. Notes to Lead-in

Henri Cartier-Bresson 亨利·卡蒂埃·布列松(August 22, 1908—August 3, 2004)是法国一位摄影艺术家,被誉为是当代摄影之父。他是早期使用35毫米相机的人之一,是抓拍艺术大师。他发展了"街头摄影"或称之为"真实生活报道"的摄影风格,对后来的几代摄影家产生了很大影响。

2. Notes to Module 1

(1) *Lethal Weapon*

《致命武器》(《轰天炮》),美国电影,上映于1987年,由理查德·唐纳导演,梅尔·吉布森,丹尼·格洛弗等主演。影片以一位金发美女从摩天大楼跳下自杀为开端,而后牵出一桩极大的走私案件。两位刑警,一位是越战特种部队出身却因突遭丧妻之痛而欲轻生的疯狂刑警玛丁·里格斯和另一位等待退休的黑人警官罗杰·玛塔夫为了追查这件事,与歹徒展开了一场斗智、斗力的比赛。

(2) *Mr. Bean's Holiday*

《憨豆先生的假期》,是"憨豆先生"系列的第二部电影,2007年3月25日在英国上映。导演是执导过处女作《绅士的启示联盟》(*The League of Gentlemen's Apocalypse*,2005)的史蒂夫·班德莱克。曾凭借"憨豆先生"系列而闻名的英国著名演员罗温·艾金森再次担任该片主演——憨豆先生。在这部影片中,憨豆先生延续了对白极少,以丰富的肢体语言和变化多端的搞笑表情来呈现剧情的特点。相比于《憨豆先生的大灾难》以美国为故事背景,在这一部影片中憨豆先生去的是法国,搞笑对象是戛纳电影节。

(3)Johannesburg Sunday Express 约翰内斯堡星期日快报。

(4)Johannesburg Star 约翰内斯堡星报。

(5)Milan

米兰,欧洲国家意大利的西北方大城,是米兰省的省会和伦巴第大区的首府,位于意大利人口最密集和发展最高的伦巴第平原上。它也是欧洲南方的重要交通要点,历史相当悠久,以观光、时尚、建筑而闻名。

(6)Sudan

苏丹。苏丹共和国位于非洲东北部,红海西岸,是非洲面积最大的国家。北邻埃及,西接利比亚、乍得、中非共和国,南毗刚果(金)、乌干达、肯尼亚,东壤埃塞俄比亚、厄立特里亚。东北濒临红海,海岸线长约720千米。

(7)*The New York Times*

《纽约时报》(*The New York Times*)有时简称为"时报"(The Times),是一份在美国纽约出版的日报,在全世界发行,有相当的影响力,美国高级报纸/严肃刊物的代表,长期以来拥有良好的公信力和权威性。由于风格古典严肃,它有时也被戏称为"灰色女士"(The Gray Lady)。它最初的名字是《纽约每日时报》(*The New York Daily Times*),创始人是亨利·贾维斯·雷蒙德和乔治·琼斯。

(8)The Pulitzer Prizes

普利策奖也称为普利策新闻奖。1917年根据美国报业巨头约瑟夫·普利策(Joseph Pulitzer)的遗愿设立,20世纪七八十年代已经发展成为美国新闻界的一项最高荣誉奖。

(9)Nissan

尼桑也叫日产。"NISSAN"的日文汉字就是"日产"。日产汽车公司创立于1933年,是日本的第二大汽车公司,是日本三大汽车制造商之一,也是世界十大汽车公司之一。日产公司的总部现设在日本东京市。

(10)*Vogue*

成立于1892年的 *Vogne* 杂志是世界上历史悠久并广受尊崇的一本时尚类杂志。杂志内容涉及时装、化妆、美容、健康、娱乐和艺术等各个方面,是一本综合性时尚生活杂志。

(11)The Museum of Modern Art in New York

纽约现代艺术博物馆(简称MOMA)。坐落在纽约市曼哈顿城中,位于曼哈顿第53街(在第五和第六大道之间),是当今世界最重要的现当代美术博物馆之一,与英国伦敦泰特美术馆、法国蓬皮杜国家文化和艺术中心等齐名。博物馆最初以展示绘画作品为主,后来展品范围渐渐扩大,包括雕塑、版画、摄影、印刷品、商业设计、电影、建筑、家具及装置艺术等项目,直到现在,其艺术品数量已达15万件之多,主要展示从19世纪末至今的艺术作品。

(12)The Pompidou Centre

巴黎蓬皮杜艺术中心坐落在巴黎拉丁区北侧、塞纳河右岸的博堡大街,当地人也常简称为"博堡",是根据法国已故总统蓬皮杜的创意而建立的。它是一座新型的、现代化的、知识、艺术与生活相结合的宝库。人们在这里可以通过现代化的技术和手段,吸收知识、欣赏艺术、丰富生活。文化中心的外部钢架林立、管道纵横,并且根据不同功能分别漆上红、黄、蓝、绿、白等颜色。因这座现代化的建筑外观极像一座工厂,故又有"炼油厂"和"文化工厂"之称。

(13) The Victoria and Albert Museum in London

伦敦维多利亚和阿尔伯特博物馆以维多利亚女王和阿尔伯特公爵命名,专门收藏美术品和工艺品,包括珠宝、家具等。它在伦敦诸多博物馆中拥有重要的地位,是因为其藏品美轮美奂所致。

3. Notes to Module 2

(1) Martin Munkacsi

马丁·慕卡西(1896—1963)匈牙利摄影家,出生于匈牙利,后加入美国国籍。他最突出的风格,就是将早期体育摄影中磨炼出的动感视觉技巧,充分融入时装拍摄之中,达到了旁人无法企及的高度。

(2) *Three Boys at Lake Tanganyika*

《坦噶尼喀湖的三个男孩》匈牙利摄影师马丁·慕卡西在1930年作品。

(3) *Life Magazine*

《生活杂志》是一本在美国家喻户晓的老牌杂志,一周发行一次,地位与《时代杂志》(*Time Magazine*)相差不远。其前身是1883年在纽约市曼哈顿发行的幽默周刊,发行社就叫做生活出版社(Life Publishing Company)。1936年,亨利·卢斯(Henry Luce)正式创立《生活杂志》,定位为新闻摄影纪实杂志,属于时代华纳公司,第一期发行日是1936年11月23日。创刊宗旨是"看见生活、看见世界"(To see life; see the world)。出版巨头时代华纳(Time Warner Inc.)在2007年3月26日正式宣布,从次月开始停止发行旗下《生活杂志》的印刷版,将内容全部转移到互联网上。这是该杂志自1936年创办以来第三次停刊。

(4) Canada Council Medal 加拿大议会奖章

(5) The Medal of Service of the Order of Canada.

加拿大勋章是加拿大的最高平民荣誉,授予那些坚持该勋章格言(Desiderantes meliorem patriam 期望有一个更好的国家)的人。该勋章创立于1967年,以认可加拿大人对国家的终生贡献。该勋章也认可非加拿大人用行动使世界更美好所作出的贡献。音乐家,政治家,艺术家,电视明星和捐助者,还有许多人都接受过这一勋章。加拿大女王,伊丽莎白二世,是该勋章的元首,在任的加拿大总督是勋章的首相和主要伙伴。1967年以来,已有超过5 000人被授予了加拿大勋章。

4. Notes to Module 3

Wedding traditions and customs vary from one country to another, but each one is special and celebrates the marriage bond of the newly weds.

Wedding Customs Around the World 世界各地婚俗

Germany: Some days before the wedding, friends and relatives bring old porcelain and kitchenware to throw on the ground in front of bride and groom. This is supposed to grant them a happy, lucky life; that's why this evening event is called Polterabend-the evening with lots of broken porcelain. The German proverb-*Scherben bringen Glück*-which can be translated as "Broken crockery brings you luck." is derived from this custom. The Polterabend often develops into an informal and casual party.

德国：在婚礼的前几天,亲朋好友会把旧瓷器和厨房用品扔在新人要经过的路上。寓意着祝福他们将开启一个愉快、幸运的生活;所以人们将发生在这个夜晚的事情称为"狂扔之夜"——一个摔破很多瓷器的夜晚。德国的谚语——碎片带来好运气——所谓"破碎的瓷器能给你带来好运气"就是来自这个风俗。扔瓷器这个风俗还经常出现在一些非正式的临时聚会上。

Early African American：Jumping the Broom In the times of slavery in this country, African American couples were not allowed to formally marry and live together. To make a public declaration of their love and commitment, a man and woman jumped over a broom into matrimony, to the beat of drums. (The broom has long held significant meaning for the various Africans, symbolizing the start of home-making for the newlywed.) In Southern Africa, the day after the wedding, the bride assisted the other women in the family in sweeping the courtyard, indicating her dutiful willingness to help her in-laws with housework till the newlyweds could move to their new home. Some African-American couples today are choosing to include this symbolic rite in their wedding ceremony. 早期非洲裔美国人：跳扫帚 在美国的黑奴时代,黑人男女是不允许正式结婚生活在一起的。为了向世人宣布他们的爱情和婚约,一对黑人男女和着鼓声的节奏,一起跳过一把扫帚。(扫帚对各种非洲人长期来都具有很重要的意义,因为它意味着新婚夫妇组成家庭的开始。)在南部非洲,新娘在婚后的第一天要帮助夫家的其他女性清扫院子,以此表明在住进自己的新家前,她愿意尽职地帮助丈夫的家人承担家务劳动。直至今日,一些美国黑人还在他们的婚礼上举行这种象征性的仪式。

England：Traditionally, the village bride and her wedding party always walk together to the church. Leading the procession：a small girl strewing blossoms along the road, so the bride's path through life will always be happy and laden with flowers. 英格兰：按照传统,乡村的新娘和参加婚礼的人们总是一起步行走向教堂。一个小姑娘走在队列最前面,她一路抛撒鲜花,预示着新娘一生的道路上也将开满鲜花,永远幸福。

Greece：The koumbaros, traditionally the groom's godfather, is an honored guest who participates in the wedding ceremony. Today, the koumbaros is very often the best man, who assists in the crowning of the couple (with white or gold crown, or with crowns made of everlasting flowers, or of twigs of love and vine wrapped in silver and gold paper), and in the circling of the altar three times. Other attendants may read *Scripture*, hold candles, pack the crowns in a special box after the ceremony. To be sure of a "sweet life", a Greek bride may carry a lump of sugar in her glove on wedding day. 希腊：通常是新郎的教父,担任婚礼上的嘉宾,现在嘉宾常常由伴郎担任,其职责是协助新郎新娘戴上花冠(花冠有白色和金色的,花冠由四季开放的鲜花,或由用金色或银色的纸包起来的象征爱情的树枝和藤编织而成)。戴上花冠后,新人们围着圣坛绕三圈。别的出席婚礼的人则朗读《圣经》,手持蜡烛,并在婚礼后将花冠放置在一个特殊的盒子里。为了确保婚后生活的甜蜜,希腊新娘在结婚那一天,可在手套里塞一块糖。

Poland：Reception guests customarily buy a dance with the bride by pining money to her veil of tucking bills into a special bridal purse to build a honeymoon fund. Luck comes of the bride who drinks a glass of wine at the celebration without spilling a drop. 波兰：出席婚礼的宾客要将钱别在新娘的面纱上或者将钱塞入新娘的一个特殊钱包里,以此来"买"得与新娘共舞一曲,而新娘则可以将这些钱积攒起来以供蜜月之用。如果新娘能够在婚礼上滴酒不漏地喝光一杯酒,幸运就会降临于新娘。

Switzerland：A pine tree, which symbolizes luck and fertility, is planted at the couple's new home. After vows, the bride's floral wreath, which symbolizes her maidenhood, is removed and set a fire by the mistress of ceremonies. It's considered lucky if it burns quickly. 瑞士：新婚夫妇的新家里会种上一棵松树,象征着运气和生育。婚礼宣誓后,象征着新娘少女身份的花环要由婚礼的女主持人取下烧掉。如果花环很快燃烧起来,这被认为是幸运的事。

Russia：Wedding guests don't only give presents—they get them! The bride gives friends and relatives favors of sweets. They give her money after the wedding. After the couple is crowned in a Russian Orthodox ceremony, they race to stand on a white rug. It is believed that whoever steps on it first will be the master of the household. 俄罗斯：婚礼的宾客不仅送给新婚夫妇礼物,他们还可以从新婚夫妇那里获得礼物。新娘送给朋友和亲戚甜点,婚礼后这些朋友和亲戚再送给新娘钱。在俄罗斯的东正教婚礼仪式上,新婚夫妇被宣布结为夫妇后,要赛跑至一块白色地毯上。人们认为谁先踏上地毯,谁就将成为一家之主。

Spain：The groom gives thirteen coins to the bride, symbolizing his ability to support and care for her. During the ceremony, she carries them in a special purse, or a young girl carries them on a pillow or handkerchief. Wedding guests dance a seguidillas manchegos at the reception, during which each guest presents the bride with a gift. 西班牙：新郎向新娘赠送 13 枚硬币以表示他有能力供养和照顾她。在婚礼上,新娘带着这些装入一个特殊的钱袋里的硬币,或放在枕头上或手绢里由一个小姑娘捧着。出席婚礼的客人跳一种叫 seguidillas manchegos 的舞蹈,其间,每个客人向新娘献上一份礼物。

III. Language Points

◆━━━━━ **Passage A** ━━━━━◆

◆Important Words◆

format［ˈfɔːmæt］*n.* the shape and size of a book, magazine, etc. 格式,大小,尺寸

e.g. 1. They brought out the newspaper in a new format.

　　　2. They publish books in all kinds of formats.

candid［ˈkændɪd］*a.* (of a photograph of a person) taken informally, esp. without the subject's knowledge 抢拍的；truthful and straight forward；frank 坦率的

e.g. 1. He took the candid shots which were much more fun than the formal group photographs.

　　　2. His responses were remarkbly candid.

reportage[ˌrepɔːˈtɑːʒ] *n.* the reporting of news or the typical style in which this is done in newspapers, or on TV and radio 报道;报告文学

e. g.　1. Readers need accurate reportage of events everyday.

　　　2. The reportage of the university in the newspaper is quite up-to-date.

financial[faɪˈnænʃl] *a.* connected with money and finance 财政的;金融的

e. g.　1. Shanghai will become the financial centre of the world.

　　　2. Most university students have no financial source except the money from their parents.

inspire[inˈspaɪə(r)] *vt.* to give sb the desire, confidence or enthusiasm to do sth well 鼓舞,激励

e. g.　1. The actors inspired the kids with their enthusiasm.

　　　2. His superb play inspired the team.

essential[ɪˈsenʃl] *a.* completely necessary; extremely important in a particular situation or for a particular activity 必不可少的;非常重要的

e. g.　1. This book is a essential reading for all nature lovers.

　　　2. Money is not essential to happiness.

enhance[ɪnˈhɑːns] *vt.* to increase or further improve the good quality, value or status of sb/sth 提高;增加;加强

e. g.　1. The images can be enhanced by using digital technology.

　　　2. This is a great opportunity to enhance the reputation of the school.

eternity[ɪˈtɜːnəti] *n.* time without end, especially life continuing without end after death 永恒

e. g.　1. Great works will sure be kept in the minds of people for eternity.

　　　2. Photography can fix one moment for eternity.

intimate[ˈɪntɪmət] *a.* having a close and friendly relationship 亲密的;密切的;private and personal 隐私的

e. g.　1. He is on intimate terms with his neighbors.

　　　2. He writes a lot about the intimate details of his life.

achieve[əˈtʃiːv] *vt.* to succeed in reaching a particular goal, status or standard, especially by making an effort for a long time 取得,获得

e. g.　1. He has finally achieved very good exam results.

　　　2. She has achieved her goal of becoming a musician.

coverage[ˈkʌvərɪdʒ] *n.* the reporting of news and sport in newspapers and on the radio and television 新闻报道；the amount of sth that sth provides；the amount or way that sth covers an area 规模；覆盖范围

e. g.　1. There is a live coverage of NBA on TV.

　　　　2. The grammar did not offer total coverage of the language.

fraction[ˈfrækʃn] *n.* a small part or amount of sth 小部分，一点儿

e. g.　1. The monthly expense is only a fraction of his income.

　　　　2. When I asked Mary to lend me some money, she hesitated for a fraction of a second.

intuition[ˌɪntjuˈɪʃn] *n.* the ability to know sth by using your feelings rather than considering the facts; an idea or a strong feeling that sth is true although you cannot explain why 直觉

e. g.　1. She always makes decisions by pure intuition.

　　　　2. Intuition told them they were going in the wrong direction.

provide sb with sth 提供；供应

e. g.　1. The lecture provided students with a lot of useful information of photography.

　　　　2. The project is to provide university graduates with jobs.

be aware of 知道

e. g.　1. The children should be aware of the danger of fire.

　　　　2. Are you aware of the need for exercising everyday?

pick up 拾起；学会

e. g.　1. When the telephone rang, I hurriedly picked up the receiver.

　　　　2. I picked up a few words of Japanese when I had a travel to Japan last year.

◆Explanation of Difficult Sentences◆

(1) He was an early adopter of 35 mm format, and a master of candid photography.

- 他是最早使用 35 毫米小型相机的摄影师之一，也是"堪的派"摄影大师。

- adopter：a person who starts using a new technology or a product as soon as it becomes available.

(2) He helped develop the "street photography" or "real life reportage" style that has influenced generations of photographers who followed.

• 在他带动下发展起来的"街头摄影"或"写实报道"风格影响了以后几代人。

（3）The anonymity that his small camera, a Leica, gave him in a crowd or during an intimate moment was essential in overcoming the formal and unnatural behaviour of subjects who were aware of being photographed.

• 小小的莱卡相机使他无论在拥挤的人群中还是在私人空间里,都不被人注意,从而避免了被摄人的拘谨状态。

• 这个句子的主干部分是 "The anonymity… was essential in overcoming…"。that his small camera, a Leica, gave him in a crowd or during an intimate moment 修饰 anonymity。"who were aware of…" 修饰 "the… of subjects"。

（4）Your eye must see a composition or an expression that life itself offers you, and you must know with intuition when to click the camera.

• 你的双眼必须能够看到生活本身所反映的一种构成或流露。而且,你必须凭着直觉知道在哪一刻按下相机的快门。

• 这是一个由 and 连接并列句。that life itself offers you 用来修饰 a composition or an expression。

Passage B

◆ Important Words ◆

accomplishment [əˈkʌmplɪʃmənt] *n.* sth good, successful or impressive that is achieved after a lot of effort and hard work 成就;成绩;完成

e.g.　1. The greatest accomplishment of parents is their children.

　　2. It is quite an accomplishment of him to pass all the exams.

unique [juˈniːk] *a.* being the only one of its kind; very special or unusual 独一无二的,仅有的

e.g.　1. A good teacher considers every student of his unique.

　　2. She is quite unique in her ways of dealing with people.

circulate [ˈsɜːkjəleɪt] *vt.* to move around within a system, or to make sth do this (使)流通;(使)循环

e.g.　1. Swimming helps the blood circulate through the muscles.

　　2. Books on health care circulate widely in China as more and more people have realized the importance of health.

definitive [dɪˈfɪnɪtɪv] *a.* considered to be the best of its kind and almost impossible to improve; final; not be able to be changed 最佳的;决定性的

e.g.　1. No one can come up with a definitive answer as to what is the best way for parents to teach their children.

2. The local government has signed a definitive agreement with the company to buy computers.

reputation [ˌrepjuˈteɪʃn] *n.* the opinion that people have about what sb/sth is like, based on what has happened in the past 名气, 名声

e. g.　1. Yaomin has acquired a reputation as a first-class basketball player in China.

　　　　2. Apple has a good reputation for its innovative products.

numerous [ˈnjuːmərəs] *a.* existing in large numbers 很多的, 许多的

e. g.　1. The two students have worked together on numerous occasions.

　　　　2. They made numerous studies to look for appropriate ways of teaching.

display [dɪsˈpleɪ] *n.* a collection of objects arranged for public viewing; *vt.* to put sth in a place where people can see it easily; to show sth to people 陈列, 展览

e. g.　1. The museum houses an informative display of rocks.

　　　　2. Shop windows display the latest fashions to attract customers.

visual [ˈvɪʒuəl] *a.* of or connected with seeing or sight 视觉的; 看得见的

e. g.　1. Artists translate their idea of the world into visual images.

　　　　2. Film is a visual art.

momentum [məʊˈmentəm] *n.* the ability to keep increasing or developing; a force that is gained by movement 动力; 势头

e. g.　1. Students should keep up the momentum for study.

　　　　2. The car gathered momentum as it rolled down the hill.

encounter [ɪnˈkaʊntə] *n.* an unexpected or casual meeting with sb or sth 遇到, 遭遇

e. g.　1. The story describes the magical encounter between a man and a dolphin.

　　　　2. I had an unexpected encounter with my schoolmate yesterday.

donate [dəʊˈneɪt] *vt.* to give money, food, clothes, etc. to sb/sth, especially a charity 捐赠, 赠送

e. g.　1. He donated thousands of dollars to the earthquake area.

　　　　2. Many people volunteer to donate their blood to the hospital.

in turn 相应地; 依次; 轮流

e. g.　1. Interest rates are cut and, in turn, house prices rose.

　　　　2. The contestants are to answer the judges' questions in turn during the speech contest.

in the belief that 深信

e. g.　1. He handed in his exam paper as soon as he finished answering all the questions in the belief that all his answers were correct.

　　2. The teacher always asks him to take part in the photo exhibition in the belief that he is the best one in the class.

◆ **Explanation of Difficult Sentences** ◆

（1）His extraordinary and unique portfolio presents the viewer with an intimate and compassionate view of humanity.

● 他独特、不同寻常的摄影作品让欣赏者读到了亲切而又善良的人性。

（2）Karsh's 1941 portrait of Winston Churchill, for example, which appeared on the cover of Life Magazine, stands as the definitive portrayal of Churchill's character.

● 卡希在 1941 年为温斯顿·邱吉尔拍摄的肖像，出现在《生活杂志》的封面上，这幅照片被认为是体现丘吉尔性格的最佳作品。

● 这个句子的主干部分是 "… portrait… stands as the definitive portrayal…"。"which appear…" 修饰前面的 portrait of Winston Churchill。

（3）Karsh also published numerous books as portfolios of his portrait photographs in the belief that a collective display gives the images a visual momentum that a single portrait alone cannot attain.

● 卡希还出版了许多肖像摄影作品集，因为他认为，(摄影作品的)集体展示能让这些肖像更具有视觉的冲击力，而单个的肖像作品是不能达到这一效果的。

● in the belief that 用来说明出版肖像摄影作品集的原因。that a single portrait alone cannot attain 修饰 a visual momentum。

（4）In each collection the portraits are accompanied by texts written by Karsh based upon his encounter with the sitter.

● 在每一系列里，卡希给每幅作品配上文字，讲述他与被摄影者相遇的经历。

● written by Karsh 和 based upon 都用来修饰 texts。

IV. Keys, Tapescripts and Text Translations

▬▬▬ Keys ▬▬▬

◆Lead-in◆

Open.

◆Module 1   Learn to Talk◆

What Shall We Do?

1. *John and Mary are talking about how to spend their weekend. Listen to the model dialogue and underline the expressions of offering and accepting suggestions.*

John: Hi, Mary, <u>would you like to</u> do something with me this weekened?

Mary: Sure. What shall we do?

John: I don't know. Do you have any ideas?

Mary: Well, <u>why don't we</u> see the photo exhibition at gallery?

John: It does sound good to me. What kind of photos can we see?

Mary: Famous photos of the Second World War.

John: That's great. <u>How about</u> starting early tomorrow?

Mary: That's a great idea. <u>Let's</u> meet at the school gate at 8:30 tomorrow morning.

John: Ok. See you tomorrow.

Mary: See you.

2. Open.

3. *John and Mary met another day after they went to the photo exhibition. Listen to the dialogue and fill in the blanks.*

   (1) Do you have any ideas?

   (2) Don't you think it might be a good idea

   (3) I'd rather not.

   (4) Shall we

   (5) why don't we

   (6) All right.

4. *Listen again and decide whether the following statements are true (T) or false (F).*

   (1) F (2) T (3) F (4) F

5. Open.

Stories of Photographers

Before You Listen

1. Open. 2. Open.

While You Listen

1. *Listen and answer the questions about Carter and Klein. Check(√) the correct box.*

Who...	Carter	Klein
1. was born in New York?	□	√
2. was once a sports photographers?	√	□
3. worked for Johannesburg Star?	√	□
4. had his first exhibition at the age of 23?	□	√
5. took drugs?	√	□
6. is accomplished in three different media?	□	√
7. has produced more than 250 TV commercials?	□	√
8. died at the age of 33?	√	□

2. *Listen again and fill in the following table about the achievements of Carter and Klein.*

	Achievements
Carter	(1) His photo of a tiny of girl became an icon of Africa's anguish. (2) He won the Pulitzer Prize.
Klein	(1) He published a book of abstract photos. (2) He worked for Vogue, as a revolutionary and talented fashion lensman. (3) His work is owned by the Museum of Modern Art in New York, the Pompidou Centre in Paris.

After You Listen

Open.

◆Module 2　Learn to Read◆

Warm-up

Open.

Passage A　Life of Henri Cartier-Bresson

Reading Comprehension

1. *Global understanding*

 (1) The passage mainly introduces the great achievements of Henri Cartier-Bresson, the father of modern photojournalism and his influence on photography.

 (2) It is a style of photography that is difficult to preplan or stage in any manner. It is the way photographers simply and honestly document life as they see it, at times adding their own interpretation to the scene.

 (3) Open.　(4) Open.

2. *Detailed understanding*

　　(1)A　(2)C　(3)B　(4)D　(5)C

Language Practice

1. Open.

2. *Match the words in Column A with the appropriate meanings in Column B.*

　　(1)j　(2)b　(3)a　(4)e　(5)g　(6)h　(7)d　(8)f　(9)i　(10)c

3. *Translate the following sentences, paying special attention to the coloured parts.*

　　(1)a. 他对人很直率。

　　　　b. 他照相时喜欢抓拍。

　　(2)a. 疼痛瞬间就消失了。

　　　　b. 有些小孩非常喜欢吃方便面。

　　(3)a. 近几年来,旅游业得到了相当大的发展。

　　　　b. 冲洗照片就是把胶卷冲印成底片。

　　(4)他推动发展的"街头摄影"或"纪实报告文学"影响了后来几代摄影人。

　　(5)摄影与绘画不同,当你摁下快门的几分之一秒,你就在创造。

Passage B　Master Portraitist：Yousuf Karsh

Reading Comprehension

1. *Global understanding*

　　(1)The passage mainly talks about Yousuf Karsh's achievements in portrait photography.

　　(2)He thinks that his photography is extraordinary and unique portfolio, which represents the viewer with an intimate and compassionate view of humanity.

2. *Detailed understanding*

　　(1)A　(2)B　(3)D　(4)A

3. *Information scanning*

Time	Things that happens to Yousuf Karsh
1908	(1)Yousuf Karsh was born.
(2)1941	He photographed Winston Churchill.
1965	He was awarded the Canada Council Medal.
1968	(3)He was awarded the Medal of Service of the Order of Canada.
(4)1987	He donated his complete collection of negatives, prints and transparencies.
1992	(5)He published *Karsh：American Legends*, 73 portraits of famous American men and women in their homes.

Language Practice

1. *Make sure you know the words in the table below. Choose the best word to complete each of the following sentences. Change the form where necessary.*

（1）accomplishment （2）encounter （3）visual （4）portrait （5）unique （6）donate

2. *Complete the following sentences by translating into English the Chinese given in brackets.*

（1）those he photographed

（2）established his international reputation

（3）based upon

（4）appeared on the cover of

（5）was awarded

◆Module 3　Culture Link◆

Quiz

1. A　2. D　3. F　4. G　5. C　6. E　7. H　8. B

◆Module 4　Scenario Link◆

Open.

■■■■■■■■■■■ Tapescripts ■■■■■■■■■■■

◆Module 1　Learn to Talk◆

What Shall We Do?

3. *John and Mary met another day after they went to the photo exhibition. Listen to the dialogue and fill in the blanks.*

John：Hi, Mary, another weekend! What's your plan?

Mary：Mm, I don't know. Do you have any ideas?

John：Don't you think it might be a good idea to see a film?

Mary：What film shall we see?

John：Let's see *Lethal Weapon*.

Mary：I'd rather not. I don't like violent films. How about going to *Mr. Bean's Holiday*? I heard it's quite a funny film.

John：Ok. Shall we go in the morning?

Mary：Oh, why don't we go in the afternoon? Then we can sleep late in the morning.

John：All right. Let's meet at 2:30 p. m. at the school gate.

Mary：Good. See you then.

John：See you.

Stories of Photographers

Kevin Carter

Kevin Carter was born in 1960 in South Africa. His parents accepted apartheid, but Kevin questioned it openly.

He first worked as a weekend sports photographer for the Johannesburg Sunday Express. In 1984, Carter moved to the Johannesburg Star and worked together with a crop of young, white photojournalists who wanted to expose the brutality of apartheid.

To relieve tension and partly to bond with gun-toting street warriors, Carter and other photojournalists smoked marijuana habitually.

In Sudan, Carter took a photo of a tiny girl chased by a vulture when she was going to eat. This photo became an icon of Africa's anguish.

Although Carter's photos of the military conflicts between white and black people eventually splashed across front pages around the world, witnessing death and murder made him feel unwell. He began to take more drugs to relieve his tension, and as a result he couldn't work as usual. His girlfriend left him. Moreover, he felt responsible for the death of his best friend, and had a deep sense of guilt.

On April 12, 1994, Carter won the Pulitzer. But some journalists in South Africa said that he won the prize by chance. Others questioned his ethics. He was also painfully aware of the photojournalist's dilemma. As a photojournalist, he always had to finish his picture before he could save people in agony. His had increasing trouble doing his work and he seemed worried about money and making ends meet.

On the morning of Wednesday, July 27, Carter poisoned himself using carbon-monoxide in his red Nissan pickup truck. He was only 33. "I'm really, really sorry," he explained in a note left on the passenger seat, "The pain of life overrode the joy to the point that joy no longer existed."

William Klein

William Klein, American photographer, painter, and filmmaker, was born in New York in 1928. He studied painting in Paris. He had his first exhibition at the age of 23. Klein is accomplished in three distinctly different medias.

While photographing artwork in Milan, he published a book of abstract photos. He achieved recognition on the photography scene with the publication of *The New York Times*, a photographic journal of his impressions there in the mid 1950s. Over the next ten years he worked for Vogue, establishing a reputation as a revolutionary and talented fashion lensman. In the 1960s, he moved to films, and received more attention overseas than in the United States, particularly for the movies *Muhammad Ali: The Greatest*, *The Little Richard Story*, and *Who Are You, Polly Magoo?*

Since 1972, Klein has produced more than 250 TV commercials, and his photo book, *Close Up* and *In and Out of Focus* secured his reputation. Klein was named one of the 30 most important photographers in the history of the medium in 1963. He has produced several books of his photographs and has exhibited in one man shows in London, Paris, and New York. His work is owned by the Museum of Modern Art in New York, the Pompidou Centre in Paris, and the Victoria and Albert Museum in London.

Text Translations

◆ Passage A ◆

亨利·卡蒂尔·布雷松

亨利·卡蒂尔·布雷松,现代新闻摄影之父。他是最早使用35毫米小型相机的摄影师之一,也是"堪的派"摄影大师,在他带动下发展起来的"街头摄影"或"写实报道"影响了以后几代人。

卡蒂尔-布雷松出生在法国,他的父亲是一名富有的纺织制造商,他母亲出生于地主和棉花商人家庭。布雷松的父母有足够的经济实力帮助他发展在摄影上面的兴趣。

卡蒂尔从匈牙利摄影记者马丁·慕卡西1931年的一张快照"三个男孩在坦噶尼喀湖"得到启示。他发现摄影可以在一瞬间凝固永恒。小小的莱卡相机使他无论在拥挤的人群中还是在私人空间里,都不被人注意,从而避免了被摄人的拘谨状态。为了尽可能的不引人注意的完成摄影,他把相机机身上明亮部分给涂黑了。

卡蒂尔-布雷松1948年在印度对甘地葬礼以及对1949年中国内战最后阶段的的报道为他赢得了国际声誉。

"摄影不像绘画,"卡蒂尔-布雷松1957年接受《华盛顿邮报》采访时说。"当你拍照时,会出现一种稍纵即逝的启发想象力的瞬间。你的双眼必须能够看到生活本身所反映的一种构成和流露。而且,你必须直觉地知道在哪一刻按下照相机的快门,这就是摄影的创造性瞬间"。

◆ Passage B ◆

肖像摄影大师:尤瑟夫·卡希

尤瑟夫·卡希(1908—2002)是20世纪摄影大师之一。他的摄影作品包括政治家、艺术家、音乐家、作家、科学家以及取得了成就的人们。他独特、不同寻常的摄影作品让欣赏者读到了亲切而又善良的人性。

尤瑟夫·卡希的肖像作品代表了20世纪政治、科学以及文化领域的重要国际人物的公众形象。这些肖像摄影都曾在公共艺术馆展出,并广泛的被杂志转载。卡希在1941年为温斯顿·邱吉尔拍摄的肖像,出现在《生活杂志》的封面上,这幅作品被认为是丘吉尔性格的最佳体现。

卡希因此建立了他在国际上的声誉。卡希的著名作品还包括威廉·索默赛特·毛姆、欧内斯特·海明威、查尔斯·戴高乐、阿尔伯特·爱因斯坦、约翰·F·肯尼迪以及马丁·路德·金等人的肖像。

卡希还出版了许多肖像摄影作品集,因为他认为,(摄影作品的)集体展示能让这些肖像更具有视觉的冲击力,而单个的肖像作品是不能达到这一效果的。在每一系列里,卡希给每幅作品配上文字,讲述他与被摄影者相遇的经历。

1965年,尤瑟夫·卡希被授予了加拿大议会奖章,1968年他又获得了加拿大勋章(加拿大公共杰出人士奖)。

1987年卡希将他在1933年至1987年的所有摄影作品的底片、照片及幻灯片都捐献给了加拿大国家档案馆,并将近100幅照片捐给了加拿大国家艺术馆。

1992年,卡希出版了《卡希:美国传说》,收集了73幅美国著名人物在家(拍摄)的肖像。其中包括伦纳德·伯恩斯坦,比尔·克林顿夫妇的肖像。

Unit 8　Playwrights

I. Background Information

Drama is a type of story acted out before an audience, often in a theater. Dramas are commonly called plays.

The person who writes the play's text is called a playwright or a dramatist.

The major elements of a play, or drama, include the characters and the plot. The characters, or the people in the story, often come into conflict with each other over something. For example, they may desire the same throne, princess, or treasure. The plot is what happens during the play and how the conflicts are settled.

In a play the characters use their words and movements to tell the story. Often the characters talk to each other. The words of their conversations are known as dialogue. Sometimes, however, a character will make a speech while alone onstage or with the other characters silent. This creates the illusion that the audience can hear the character's thoughts. That kind of speech is called a soliloquy. Occasionally a character will speak directly to the audience. This is called an aside.

A playwright might write dialogue that sounds natural, or how people of a particular time and place actually talk. Or the dialogue may be very formal. For instance, sometimes the characters' words are written in poetry. In some dramas the characters may sing or chant their words.

The playwright also writes short instructions, called stage directions, in the text. Some stage directions tell the actors what to do, such as when and where to enter the stage. Other directions may describe what a character looks like. They may also indicate the time and place of the action. The play's designers use these descriptions to create the scenery, costumes, and lighting.

II. Notes

1. Notes to Lead-in

(1) *Much Ado about Nothing*

《无事生非》是莎士比亚创作的喜剧,在 1600 年首次出版。它与现代浪漫喜剧在风格上有相同之处,至今仍是最受欢迎的莎翁剧作之一。此剧首五幕围绕:Claudio 和 Hero、Benedick 和 Beatrice 两对情人来展开。他们在恋爱过程中分别因为各自的傲气十足和小人的挑拨而引出一段段精彩的插曲。其结局虽然幸福美满,两对新人双双踏上红地毯,但其间的过程却一波三折,引人入胜。

(2) TNT Theatre

英国 TNT 剧院创立于 1980 年,是世界级国际巡演剧团,曾获得慕尼黑比奈尔节、爱丁堡戏剧节、德黑兰艺术节大奖和新加坡政府奖等多项大奖。TNT 剧院不仅在英国本土声名显赫,而且是全球巡演国家和场次最多的英语剧团——几乎占据了德国全部英语话剧市场,也是在法国、日本和俄罗斯演出最多的英语剧团。TNT 剧院倡导戏剧激发观众的想象力,让观众成为戏剧的参与者而非旁观者,致力于在戏剧中融入多种艺术形式,每个剧目都邀请顶级作曲家为其量身创作音乐,因此作品中有很重的音乐和舞蹈元素。TNT 剧院从 2000 年开始创作莎士比亚的系列作品,包括《哈姆雷特》《麦克白》《仲夏夜之梦》《罗密欧与朱丽叶》《驯悍记》等,迄今已在全球 20 多个国家演出 1 000 余场。

（3）老舍

老舍(1899 年 2 月 3 日—1966 年 8 月 24 日),本名舒庆春,字舍予,北京满族正红旗人,原姓舒觉罗氏,中国现代著名作家。老舍有"文学语言大师"的称号,其中包括 300 多万字的小说,42 部戏剧,约 300 首旧体诗等。他的作品多为悲剧,作品的语言以北京方言为主,风格幽默。他的代表作是小说《骆驼祥子》和话剧《茶馆》。

（4）曹禺

曹禺(1910 年 9 月 24 日—1996 年 12 月 13 日)本名万家宝,字小石,是中国现代剧作家以及戏剧教育家,他被称为"中国的莎士比亚"。曹禺的代表作包括《雷雨》《原野》《日出》《北京人》。

（5）Oscar Wilde

奥斯卡·王尔德(1854 年 10 月 16 日—1900 年 11 月 30 日),爱尔兰作家、诗人、剧作家,英国唯美主义艺术运动的倡导者。

（6）Eugene O'Neill

尤金·奥尼尔(1888 年 10 月 16 日—1953 年 11 月 27 日),美国著名剧作家,表现主义文学的代表作家。主要作品有《琼斯皇》《毛猿》《天边外》《悲悼》等,于 1936 年获诺贝尔文学奖。

（7）Arthur Miller

阿瑟·米勒(1915 年 10 月 17 日—2005 年 2 月 10 日)是一位美国剧作家,生于纽约市,他以剧作《推销员之死》《熔炉》,以及在 1956 年与玛丽莲·梦露的婚姻而闻名。

2. Notes to Module 1

（1）*The Peony Pavilion*

《牡丹亭》,原名《还魂记》,又名《杜丽娘慕色还魂记》是明代剧作家汤显祖的代表作,创作于 1598 年,描写了大家闺秀杜丽娘和书生柳梦梅的生死之恋。与《紫钗记》《南柯记》《邯郸记》并称为"玉茗堂四梦"。

（2）Tang Xianzu

汤显祖(1550 年—1616 年),中国明代末期戏曲剧作家、文学家。字义仍,号海若、清远道人,晚年号若士、茧翁,江西临川人。

（3）Princeton

普林斯顿大学,又译普林斯敦大学,位于美国新泽西州的普林斯顿,是美国一所著名的私立研究型大学,8 所常春藤盟校之一。学校于 1746 年在新泽西州伊丽莎白镇创立,是美国殖民时期第 4 所成立的高等教育学院,当时名为"新泽西学院",1756 年迁至普林斯顿,并于 1896 年正式改名为普林斯顿大学。

（4）George Pierce Baker

乔治·皮尔斯·贝克(1866—1935),在剧本撰写领域有影响力的教育家。他 1887 年毕业于哈佛大学,并于 1888 年至 1924 年间在哈佛大学教授英语。由于无法说服哈佛大学颁发戏剧创作的学位,他在 1925 年调动到耶鲁大学任教直至 1933 年退休。

（5）Harvard

哈佛大学,是一所位于美国马萨诸塞州剑桥的私立大学,常春藤盟校成员之一。1636 年由马萨诸塞州殖民地立法机关立案成立,迄今已是美国历史最悠久的高等学府,也是北美第一间和最古老的法人机构（corporation）。同位于剑桥市,该校与临近的麻省理工学院在世界上享有一流大学的声誉、财富和影响力,在英语系大学的排名中尤其突出。另外,哈佛也是全世界产生最多罗德奖学金（有"全球本科生诺贝尔奖"之称）得主的大学。

（6）Provincetown 普罗温斯敦,是位于美国马萨诸塞州的一个城镇。

（7）Massachusetts

马萨诸塞州是美国的一州,正式名称为"马萨诸塞联邦"（Commonwealth of Massachusetts）,是美国东北部新英格兰地区的一部分。在中文中,通常简称"麻州"或"马萨诸塞州"。

（8）Broadway

百老汇大道,为纽约市重要的南北向道路,南起巴特里公园（Battery Park）,由南向北纵贯曼哈顿岛。由于此路两旁分布着为数众多的剧院,是美国戏剧和音乐剧的重要发扬地,因此成为了戏剧及音乐剧的代名词。

（9）The Nobel Prize for Literature

诺贝尔文学奖,是阿尔弗雷德·诺贝尔设立的诺贝尔奖中的一个奖项。诺贝尔在遗嘱中说奖金的一部分应该"奖给在文学界创作出具有理想倾向的最佳作品的人"。诺贝尔文学奖由瑞典学院颁奖。

（10）Boston

波士顿是美国马萨诸塞州的首府和最大城市,也是新英格兰地区的最大城市。该市位于美国东北部大西洋沿岸,创建于 1630 年,是美国最古老、最有文化价值的城市之一。波士顿是美国革命期间一些重要事件的发生地点,曾经是一个重要的航运港口和制造业中心。今天,该市是高等教育和医疗保健的中心,并被认为是一个全球性城市或世界性城市。

3. Notes to Module 2

（1）Stratford-upon-Avon

埃文河畔斯特拉特福镇,英国英格兰沃里克郡埃文河畔斯特拉特福区的一个小镇,著名剧作家威廉·莎士比亚的故乡。

（2）Lord Chamberlain's Men

张伯伦勋爵剧团,该剧团是以资助它的贵族的名字命名的,莎士比亚是其合伙人,后来更名为国王剧团。

（3）*Hamlet*

《哈姆雷特》,又名《王子复仇记》,是莎士比亚的一部悲剧作品,习惯上将本剧与《麦克白》《李尔王》《奥赛罗》一起并称为莎士比亚的"四大悲剧"。

（4）*King Lear*

《李尔王》,莎士比亚最著名的悲剧之一,李尔王是英国的一个古老传说,故事本身发生在公元前 8 世纪左右。关于这位国王的史记、诗歌和剧作在莎士比亚时代以前已存在。

(5) *Macbeth*

《麦克白》,莎士比亚最短的悲剧,也是他最受欢迎的作品之一。此部作品经常在世界各地的专业和社区剧院上演。这出戏剧是典型的因权力的渴望而背弃朋友的故事。而历史上麦克白真有其人,他是公元11世纪欧洲苏格兰王国的国王,在位 17 年。

(6) *A Midsummer Night's Dream*《仲夏夜之梦》,莎士比亚创作的浪漫喜剧。

(7) *As You Like It*《皆大欢喜》,莎士比亚于 1599 年创作的一部喜剧。

(8) *The Taming of the Shrew*《驯悍记》,莎士比亚早期的一部喜剧。

(9) *Henry IV*《亨利四世》,莎士比亚著名的历史剧,主要写亨利四世前后,贵族叛乱及平叛的过程。

(10) *Richard II*《理查二世》,莎士比亚创作的一部历史剧。

(11) Roxbury 罗克斯伯利镇,位于美国康涅狄格州。

(12) Connecticut 康涅狄格州,是美国东北部的一州,也是新英格兰区域中最南的一州。

(13) New York Drama Critics' Circle Awards

纽约戏剧评论界奖,是除普利策奖、托尼奖之外的又一项重要戏剧奖。每年 5 月由除了《纽约时报》以外的所有纽约报纸的评论家评选出。目前该奖设有最佳戏剧(话剧)、最佳音乐剧、最佳外国戏剧、最佳新剧和特别奖等奖项。

(14) Tony Awards

托尼奖中文全称为安东尼特·佩瑞奖,英文全称为 Antoinette Perry Awards for Excellence in Theatre。托尼奖由美国戏剧协会为纪念该协会创始人之一——安东尼特·佩瑞女士而设立。托尼奖设立于 1947 年,被视为美国话剧和音乐剧的最高奖,共设 21 个奖项,获提名剧目均是在百老汇各剧院演出的剧目。1947 年 4 月 6 日,第一届托尼奖在纽约市著名的华尔道夫大饭店揭幕,并由佩瑞的好友兼合作伙伴、美国戏剧协会主席布鲁克·佩贝顿主持。当时的决策机构 6 人委员会聘请了 15 位专家,通过秘密投票方式选出了获奖人。从那之后,托尼奖与百老汇的艺术声望、美学地位和票房收入等一起,成为全球舞台艺术的焦点。

(15) John F. Kennedy Center for the Performing Arts

肯尼迪表演艺术中心位于美国首都华盛顿西北,是华盛顿著名的文化活动中心。该中心 1966 年破土动工,1971 年正式对外开放。它以美国前总统肯尼迪的名字命名,以纪念这位在 1963 年 11 月遇刺身亡的年轻总统。肯尼迪表演艺术中心是一座由 3 700 吨白色大理石建成的方形建筑物,长 630 英尺,宽 300 英尺。

(16) Washington, D. C.

华盛顿,哥伦比亚特区,美利坚合众国的首都,位于美国东北部,靠近维吉尼亚州和马里兰州。哥伦比亚特区(District of Columbia,缩写:D. C.)是 1790 年做为首都而设置,由联邦政府直接管辖的特别行政区。

4. Notes to Module 3

British people are often stereotyped as being cold and reserved. However, this is often not because they are being deliberately unfriendly, but because they do not wish to invade other peoples' privacy. In fact, British people can be very warm and friendly.

British people are usually very polite, using "please" and "thank you" a lot, which you may not be used to. In addition, the British have a tendency to be very self-critical and apologetic. You will find that the words "sorry" and "excuse me" are also used frequently.

The British often have difficulty saying what they really mean, for example refusing a request, or making a critical comment, for fear of causing offence or upset. If, in your culture, it is usual for people to be very open and direct when expressing their opinions, you may have some difficulties understanding what British people really mean. If you are in any doubt, ask.

British people have a strong sense of humour which can be very ironic and sometimes hard for foreigners to understand.

The British generally have a reputation for punctuality. In both schools and in the workplace, time-keeping is important. Since Britons are so time conscious, the pace of life may seem very rushed. In Britain, people make great effort to arrive on time. It is often considered impolite to arrive even a few minutes late. If you are unable to keep an appointment, it is expected that you call the person you are meeting.

III. Language Points

▰▰▰▰ Passage A ▰▰▰▰

◆ Important Words ◆

praise[preɪz]*vt.* to express your approval or admiration for sb/sth 称赞;赞美

e.g.　1. She praised his cooking.

　　　2. He praised his team for their performance.

disease[dɪˈziːz]*n.* an illness affecting humans, animals or plants, often caused by infection 疾病

e.g.　1. heart/liver/kidney disease

　　　2. It is not known what causes the disease.

official[əˈfɪʃl]*n.* a person who is in a position of authority in a large organization 要员;官员

e.g.　a bank/company/court/government official

spread[spred]*n.* an increase in the amount or number of sth that there is, or in the area that is affected by sth 传播;散布

e.g.　1. Handwashing is an easy way to prevent the spread of disease.

　　　2. Shut doors to delay the spread of fire.

category[ˈkætəɡəri]*n.* a group of people or things with particular features in common 种类;类别

e.g.　1. Students over 25 fall into a different category.

　　　2. The results of this survey can be divided into three main categories.

tragedy ['trædʒədi] *n.* a serious play with a sad ending, especially one in which the main character dies 悲剧;a very sad event or situation, especially one that involves death 悲惨的事;不幸

e. g.　1. Tragedy struck the family when their three-year-old daughter was hit by a car and killed.

　　　　2. The whole affair ended in tragedy.

comedy ['kɒmədi] *n.* a play or film/movie that is intended to be funny, usually with a happy ending 喜剧;an amusing aspect of sth 滑稽;幽默

e. g.　1. He acted in a highly successful TV comedy.

　　　　2. He didn't appreciate the comedy of the situation.

be involved with 耗费很多时间;关注;涉及

e. g.　1. She was deeply involved with the local hospital.

　　　　2. He has been actively involved with the church for years.

fall into 可以分成;能够分成

e. g.　1. My talk falls naturally into three parts.

　　　　2. Many illnesses fall into the category of stress-related illnesses.

retire from 退职;退休

e. g.　1. She was forced to retire early from teaching because of ill health.

　　　　2. My father retired from his position as librarian last year.

◆ Explanation of Difficult Sentences ◆

(1) William Shakespeare is often praised as the world's greatest playwright.

● 威廉·莎士比亚通常被誉为全世界最卓越的剧作家。

● be praised as 是被动语态形式,意思是"被称赞为,被誉为"。

(2) In that year, a disease called the black plague devastated the city.

● 那一年,被称为"黑死病"的疾病侵袭了这座城市。

● called the black plague 这部分是以过去分词短语作后置定语,修饰名词 disease,表示被动。理解为 "被称为'黑死病'的疾病"。

(3) Shakespeare then turned to writing poetry.

● 莎士比亚由此转向诗歌的创作。

● 其中的 turn to sth/doing sth 表示把(注意力等)转向,如:More and more people turn to computer science. 愈来愈多的人从事计算机科学研究。

(4) Officials closed the theaters and other public places to stop its spread.

- 为了防止这一疾病的传播,官员们下令关闭了剧院及其他公共场所。
- spread 一词在该句中的词性为名词。此外,该词还常作为动词使用。如:

The disease spreads easily. 这种疾病容易传播。

Within weeks, his confidence had spread throughout the team.

短短几个星期,他的信心感染了全体队员。

(5) Along with acting and writing, Shakespeare also was involved with the business side of thea-ter.

- 除了表演与写作,莎士比亚还参与剧院的经营业务。
- the business side of the theater 指的是剧院的业务方面。如:More input on the technical side would help. 若在技术方面多些投入会更好。

Passage B

◆ Important Words ◆

critic ['krɪtɪk] n. a person who expresses opinions about the good and bad qualities of books, music, etc. 批评家;评论家;评论员

e.g. 1. The critics loved the movie.

2. He is a famous music critic.

dramatize ['dræmətaɪz] vt. to present a book, an event, etc. as a play or a film/movie 将……改编成剧本;将……搬上(舞台或银幕)to make sth seem more exciting or important than it really is 使戏剧化

e.g. 1. Jane Austen's "Emma" was dramatized on television recently.

2. Don't worry too much about what she said—She tends to dramatize things.

emotional [ɪ'məʊʃənl] a. connected with people's feelings 感情的;情绪的

e.g. 1. Mothers are often the ones who provide emotional support for the family.

2. Ann suffered from some emotional problems.

average ['ævərɪdʒ] a. ordinary; not special 普通的;calculated by adding several amounts to-gether, finding a total, and dividing the total by the number of amounts 平均的

e.g. 1. I am just an average sort of student.

2. The car runs at an average speed of 100 miles per hour.

demonstrate[ˈdemənstreɪt]*vt.* to show by your actions that you have a particular quality, feeling or opinion 表达;说明

e. g.   1. You need to demonstrate more self-control.

2. We want to demonstrate our commitment to human rights.

explore[ɪkˈsplɔː(r)]*vt.* to examine sth completely or carefully in order to find out more about it 探究;探索

e. g.   1. These ideas will be explored in more detail in chapter 7.

2. I am going to explore the possibility of a part-time job.

unreasonable[ʌnˈriːznəbl]*a.* not fair, expecting too much 不合理的;期望过高的

e. g.   1. It would be unreasonable to expect somebody to come at such short notice.

2. Your request is completely unreasonable.

accuse[əˈkjuːz]*vt.* to say that you believe someone is guilty of a crime or of doing sth bad 指责;控告

e. g.   1. He was accused of murder.

2. Smith accused her of lying.

innocent[ˈɪnəsnt]*a.* not guilty of a crime, etc.; not having done sth wrong 无辜的;清白的

e. g.   1. She was found innocent of any crime.

2. They punished an innocent man.

horrible[ˈhɒrəbl]*a.* very bad or unpleasant; used to describe sth that you do not like 令人震惊的;恐怖的

e. g.   1. The weather is horrible today.

2. The coffee tastes horrible.

crime[kraɪm]*n.* activities that involve breaking the law 犯罪活动;不法行为

e. g.   1. We moved here ten years ago because there was very little crime.

2. Stores spend more and more on crime prevention every year.

honour[ˈɒnə(r)]*vt.* to give public praise, an award or a title to sb for sth they have done 给予表扬(或奖励、头衔、称号)

e. g.   1. He was honoured with an award for excellence in teaching.

2. Two firefighters have been honoured for their courage.

stop sb from doing sth 阻止某人做某事;阻碍某人做某事;阻拦

e. g.   1. There is nothing to stop you form accepting the offer.

        2. You can't stop people from saying what they think.

◆ Explanation of Difficult Sentences ◆

(1) Several plays by Arthur Miller will probably be performed for many years to come.

- 在未来的许多年中,亚瑟·米勒的一些戏剧作品很可能仍将上演。

- plays by Arthur Miller 指的是由米勒创作的戏剧作品。

many years to come 未来的许多年。

(2) That is because critics say Miller was able to dramatize the emotional pain that average people suffer in their daily lives.

- 这是因为剧评家称米勒能够在其剧作中将寻常百姓日常生活中的精神痛苦表现出来。

- that average people suffer in their daily lives 是一个由 that 引导的定语从句,修饰名词 pain。

(3) The main character is a man whose dreams of success in business have died。

- 该剧中,主角追求事业成功的梦想破灭了。

- whose dreams of success in business have died 是一个由 whose 引导的定语从句,修饰名词 man。

(4) In *The Crucible*, for example, he shows what happens when unreasonable dislike and fear cause people to accuse innocent people of horrible crimes.

- 例如,在《萨勒姆的女巫》这一剧作中米勒讲述了不近人情的厌恶和恐惧使得人们指控无辜者犯了可怕的罪行。

- when unreasonable dislike and fear cause people to accuse innocent people of horrible crimes 这部分是一个以 when 一词引导的状语从句。accuse sb of sth 意思为指控、谴责某人犯了某事。

IV. Keys, Tapescripts and Text Translations

▬▬▬▬ Keys ▬▬▬▬

◆ Lead-in ◆

open.

◆ Module 1   Learn to Talk ◆

Talking About Similarities and Differences

1. *Susan meets Jay who just came back from America. Listen to the model dialogue and underline the expressions used to talk about similarities and differences.*

Susan: Hey! Jay! What's up?

Jay: Oh, I actually just got back from Los Angeles!

Susan: How was your trip?

Jay: It was great! But I picked up some American words, and now I forget which ones to use!

Susan: Why? Are they different from British words?

Jay: Yeah. It's so confusing! You know there are so many differences. It's almost a completely different language sometimes!

Susan: Really? I thought they were the same.

Jay: You know the lift over there?

Susan: Yeah?

Jay: That's an elevator in American English.

Susan: Oh really?

Jay: You know in the States, you don't go to watch a film.

Susan: You "watch a movie"?

Jay: Exactly! You got it!

2. Open.

3. (1)drama   (2)playwight   (3)common   (4)same   (5)both
   (6)difference (7)writing   (8)character   (9)views   (10)play

4. Open.

Story of a Playwright

Before You Listen

1. Open.   2. Open.

While You Listen

1. *Listen and decide whether the following statements are true (T) or false (F).*
   (1)F   (2)T   (3)T   (4)F   (5)T   (6)T

2. *Listen to the story of O'Neill again and rearrange the events in the correct time order.*
   (4) → (6) → (5) → (2) → (1) → (3)

After You Listen

Open.

◆Module 2   Learn to Read◆

Warm-up

Open.

Passage A　The World's Greatest Playwright：William Shakespeare

Reading Comprehension

1. *Global understanding*

　　(1) The passage mainly introduces Shakespeare's life and his plays.

　　(2) The tone of the passage is matter-of-fact.

2. *Detailed understanding*

　　(1) B　(2) C　(3) A　(4) B

Language Practice

1. *Word search puzzle：find the new words from Passage A hidden within the puzzle.*

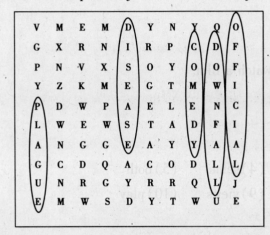

2. *Make sure you know the words in the table below. Choose a word to complete each of the following sentences. Change the form where necessary.*

　　(1) spread　　(2) praised　　(3) involved　　(4) tragedy

　　(5) official　　(6) categories　　(7) devastate　　(8) disease

3. *Translate the following sentences into English，using the expressions in the brackets.*

　　(1) Readers praised this book as the best book of the year.

　　(2) She lost her job along with hundreds of others.

　　(3) She is deeply involved with teaching.

　　(4) My talk falls into three parts.

　　(5) She retired from teaching when she was 60.

Passage B　One of the Greatest American Playwrights of the 20th Century：Arthur Miller

Reading Comprehension

1. *Global understanding*

　　Paragraph 1：b　　Paragraph 2：a　　Paragraph 3：c

2. *Detailed understanding*

　　(1) D　　(2) B　　(3) A

3. *Information matching*

Name	Arthur Miller
Born	(1) New York City , 1915
Died	(2) Roxbury, Connecticut, 2005
Occupation	(3) playwright
Nationality	American
Notable works	(4) *Death of a Salesman*, *The Crucible*, *All My Sons*, *A View from the Bridge*, *After the Fall*
Notable Awards	(5) a Pulitzer Prize, New York Drama Critics' Circle Awards, Tony awards, and Lifetime Achievement Award by John F. Kennedy Center.

Language Practice

1. *Match the words in Column A with the appropriate meanings in Column B.*

(1) e　(2) g　(3) b　(4) d　(5) h　(6) a　(7) c　(8) f

2. *Complete the following sentences by translating into English the Chinese given in brackets.*

(1) an average sort of student　　(2) You need to demonstrate

(3) explored on foot　　(4) are not unreasonable

(5) crime prevention

◆Module 3　Culture Link◆

1. *Manners are considered important in British culture. Are the following behaviours acceptable in Britain? Tick the acceptable ones.*

☑ Standing in line and waiting for your turn.

☐ Asking a lady her age.

☑ Shaking someone's right hand with your own right hand when you are first introduced to someone.

☐ Talking loudly in public.

☑ Taking your hat off when you go indoors (men only).

☑ Saying "Excuse Me" if someone is blocking your way.

☐ Spiting in the street.

☑ Covering your mouth with your hand when yawning or coughing.

☑ Driving on the left side of the road.

☑ Holding the door open for each other.

☐ Greeting people with a kiss.

☐ Picking nose in public.

2. *How much do you know about British Character? Read each of the following questions and choose the answers from the box below.*

(1) D　(2) B　(3) A　(4) C

◆Module 4　Scenario Link◆

Open.

━━━━━━━ **Tapescripts** ━━━━━━━

◆Module 1　Learn to Talk◆

Talking About Similarities and Differences

3. *Listen to two students talking about famous playwrights and fill in the missing words.*

A: The drama last night was a thriller, wasn't it?

B. Yes. *The Peony Pavilion* is Tang Xianzu's masterpiece, and I'm truly crazy about it.

A: I can't help thinking about Shakespeare, the greatest playwright ever.

B: Well, Tang is thought to have something in common with Shakespeare.

A: Tell me more about it.

B: Tang of the Ming Dynasty lived in roughly the same era as Shakespeare. They both created a lot of impressive figures in their works. And…

A: And I know they both enjoy wide popularity around the world!

B: True. But there is still much difference between them in writing styles, character features, and views of love, etc.

A: I got you.

B: You know what?

A: What?

A: Students of the English department are putting on a Shakespeare's play tonight. Why don't we go watch it?

B: Good idea!

Stories of a Playwright

　　Eugene Gladstone O'Neill was born on October 16, 1888, in New York City. His father was a well known actor. As a child O'Neill traveled with his father's company until he was 8, when he went to a private school. In 1906 he entered Princeton but left at the end of his freshman year. From 1914–1915 he studied dramatic writing with George Pierce Baker at Harvard. He wrote the one-act plays that were presented by the Provincetown Players in Massachusetts. In 1920 O'Neill's first full-length play, *Beyond the Horizon*, was produced on Broadway. It won the Pulitzer Prize. In 1922 *Anna Christie* won another, and in 1928 *Strange Interlude* won a third. In 1936 he was the first American dramatist to win the Nobel Prize for Literature. The last ten years of O'Neill's life were filled with frustration. He and his third wife lived in a hotel in Boston, where he died on November 27, 1953. His final play, the autobiographical *Long Day's Journey into Night*, published posthumously in 1956, won a fourth Pulitzer Prize.

Text Translations

◆ Passage A ◆

全世界最卓越的剧作家：威廉·莎士比亚

威廉·莎士比亚通常被誉为全世界最卓越的剧作家。尽管他生活在 400 多年前，但是人们至今仍旧在研究和欣赏他的作品。

1564 年，威廉·莎士比亚出生在英国的埃文河畔斯特拉特福镇。他有三个弟弟和两个妹妹。

1592 年前，莎士比亚在伦敦从事写作和表演。那一年，被称为"黑死病"的疾病侵袭了这座城市。为了防止这一疾病的传播，官员们下令关闭了剧院及其他公共场所。莎士比亚由此转向诗歌的创作。

1594 年，伦敦的剧院再度开放。此前，莎士比亚已加入了张伯伦勋爵剧团。这一剧团常常为王族表演剧目。除了表演与写作，莎士比亚还参与管理剧院的业务，他也变得富有。

在 20 年中，莎士比亚创作了 37 个剧本。他的剧作分为三大类：悲剧、喜剧和历史剧。悲剧讲述剧中主要人物的衰落。莎士比亚最著名的悲剧有《哈姆雷特》《李尔王》《麦克白》等。喜剧剧情幽默、结局欢喜。他的喜剧作品包括《仲夏夜之梦》《皆大欢喜》《驯悍记》等。莎士比亚的历史剧主要人物是英国的国王，作品包括《亨利四世》和《理查德二世》等。

大约在 1610 年，莎士比亚从剧院退休，回到他的家乡埃文河畔斯特拉特福镇。1616 年 4 月 23 日逝世。

◆ Passage B ◆

20 世纪美国最杰出的剧作家之一：阿瑟·米勒

阿瑟·米勒于 1951 年出生在美国，2005 年在其康涅狄格州鲁克斯伯利镇的家中去世。60 年来，他创作了一部又一部的剧作。许多的剧评家认为阿瑟·米勒是 20 世纪美国最杰出的剧作家之一。

在未来的许多年中，他的一些作品很可能仍将上演。这是因为剧评家称米勒能够在其剧作中将寻常百姓日常生活中的精神痛苦表现出来。一个剧评家认为米勒是"平民百姓的活动家"。这一点在米勒的代表作《推销员之死》中有很好的体现，该剧中，主角追求事业成功的梦想破灭了。但米勒对平民百姓的关注并没有使他停止对社会问题的探究。例如，在《萨勒姆的女巫》这一剧作中米勒讲述了不近人情的厌恶和恐惧使得人们指控无辜者犯了可怕的罪行。米勒的著名剧作还包括《吾子吾弟》《桥上一瞥》《堕落之后》等。

米勒获得了许多奖，包括一座普利策奖、纽约戏剧评论界奖和托尼奖。1984 年，肯尼迪表演艺术中心授予他戏剧终身成就奖。